DOES JACOB'S TROUBLE WEAR A CROSS?

DOES JACOB'S TROUBLE WEAR A CROSS?

The Ancient Legacy of Christian Anti-Semitism

by

Randall A. Weiss

Published by

Excellence In Christian Books

EICB

P.O. Box 668
Dyer, Indiana
46311-0668 U.S.A.

Excellence In Christian Books
EICB

First printing January, 1995
Copyright © 1995 Randall A. Weiss
ISBN 1-57376-000-5
****

SPECIAL NOTE: Institutional discounts will be granted to teachers and academic institutions intending to promote Judeo-Christian values while healing wounds between Jews and Christians. This is the goal of Excellence In Christian Books, and the media division Excellence In Christian Broadcasting.

Published by: EICB, P.O. Box 668, Dyer IN 46311-0668

<u>Dedication</u>

This book is lovingly dedicated

to my precious bride.

Adrienne,

I love you!

Thanks for letting me study

to show myself approved.

TABLE OF CONTENTS

FOREWORD

Wake up Christians! If taken in the spirit of truth and love (the same spirit in which it was written), this book will be a very clear trumpet blast that will cause sleepy Gentile Christians, like I was, to stir themselves and open their willfully closed eyes.

Sleepy Gentile Christians with willfully closed eyes are those who while not anti-Semitic have simply not taken the time to find out that there has been a long history of hatred by so-called *Christians* against the Jewish people. Even the *Sleepy Gentile Christians with willfully closed eyes* know about the atrocities of Adolf Hitler, and they condemn such hellishly inspired brutality. But it will surprise many Christians to discover that some *real Christians* have also been anti-Semitic as well.

For those who think that their anti-Semitic behavior is justified by their interpretations of the New Testament, this book is more than a trumpet blast. It carries within its pages the same hot breath of John the Baptist who said in no uncertain terms: "Repent."

Randy Weiss, a Jewish/Christian scholar, has done an excellent job of compiling a very large amount of information and putting it into a clear, readable style. Mr. Weiss has given the Christian Church (made up of all people groups, Jews and Gentiles) a very potent medicine that if taken with an honest and open heart, will *begin* to heal the ignorance (and hatred) of many Christians, and, we hope, the pain of many Jews.

Rick Walston, Ph.D.

President of Faraston Theological Seminary

THE GROWTH OF
ANTI-SEMITISM
IN THE CHURCH OF THE
OLD WORLD

Alas! for that day is great,
so that none is like it:
it is even the time of Jacob's trouble;
but he shall be saved out of it. (30:7)

Jeremiah the Prophet

CHAPTER I

THE QUESTION

DOES JACOB'S TROUBLE WEAR A CROSS!

Yes! "Jacob's Trouble" has worn the cross. This book will show that Christian history is littered with the debris of anti-Semitism. It may be apparent that certain biases exist within this research. If it is not apparent, honesty demands that they be admitted since they will inevitably effect the tone and content of the conclusions. Every scholarly effort should presuppose a certain level of objectivity. When this objectivity is lacking the value of the work can be called into question. I call my own conclusions into question so that they will not be accepted without fair warning. With this caveat aside, I am confident that the preponderance of historical evidence will lead to an inescapable conclusion that rises above any bias I may hold.

DOES JACOB'S TROUBLE WEAR A CROSS?

To avoid sounding enigmatic, permit an explanation of the title, "Does Jacob's Trouble Wear a Cross?" Jeremiah spoke to the Children of Israel during the early part of the seventh century BCE.[1] This was an era of national disobedience. In chapter 30 of Jeremiah's prophecy, he foretold of a "time of Jacob's trouble." Future national judgment for Israel's sins were forthcoming. Jeremiah spoke of a time of deep suffering (which many believe occurred during the Babylonian exile of 586 BCE). His message was sobering but his words also brought hope. Jeremiah foretold of a great future deliverance. God reminded Israel of His eternal committed love. He said, "For I am with thee, saith the LORD, to save thee" (Jer. 30:11).[2] Jeremiah expressed God's intentions to the Jews. He reminded them, "And ye shall be My people, And I will be your God" (Jer. 30: 22). The Bible clearly proposes that God has chosen the Children of

---

[1] As preferred by some Jewish writers, the abbreviations BCE and CE will be used respectively indicating "Before the Common Era" and "Common Era" in place of BC and AD, except as used by other writers in quotes.

[2] Unless otherwise noted, all Hebrew Bible (Old Testament) Scripture references used are from *The Holy Scriptures According to the Masoretic Text*, (The Jewish Publication Society of America, Philadelphia, 1955). Unless otherwise noted, all New Testament Scripture references are from the New King James Version. King James Version references will be identified by KJV. New International Version references will be identified by NIV.

Israel to be His people. He has not changed His mind or broken His promise. In the Sinai wilderness He explained His reasons for choosing the Jews.

> The LORD thy God hath chosen thee to be His own treasure, out of all peoples that are upon the face of the earth. The LORD did not set His love upon you, nor choose you, because ye were more in number . . . but because the LORD loved you, and because He would keep the oath which He swore unto your fathers (Deut. 7:6-8).

The Jews are Undeniably Chosen

God loves the Jewish people. If the Bible is accepted as God's Word to believers, the chosenness of the Children of Israel is undeniable. God has expressed His love for the Children of Israel, and He has called the Church to share His love. This research will show that instead of love, jealousy and hatred have often been evident. I intend to prove that the Church has failed insofar as it has primarily offered judgment, rather than redemption, to the Jewish people. I believe many Jews ignore the gospel claims because Christians ignore the gospel call. True Christian service transcends "go and tell," though Christians do preach the gospel. They ignore the call to show and tell. Modern Jews have rarely been shown the love of Jesus, they have only been told. For that lack, Jews do not often experience the love of Jesus because Gentile Christianity

DOES JACOB'S TROUBLE WEAR A CROSS?

has generally offered punishment, not love. As the question was answered in the first line of this book, "Yes! Jacob's trouble has <u>worn</u> a cross. I am personally convinced that Jacob's hope <u>bore</u> one. Nonetheless, this book is <u>not</u> about Jewish evangelism. This book is about Christian error. As a Jew, I rarely experienced the love of the Church yet, as a Christian, I am grateful for the love of Jesus. This book will point out the difference.

I have desired to perform research that rises above the level of my own subjective weaknesses. Still, it may help my reader more ably discern the truth, if he can identify the experience of the writer within the research. However, facts alone will serve to prove or disprove the premise of this book, which is: Christianity <u>does</u> have a legacy of sinful, willful, violent anti-Semitism.[3]

---

[3] It is necessary to explain the specific choice of terminology. In this book, anti-Semitism has been used throughout as an expression referring specifically to hostility against Judaism, and Jewish people. Anti-Judaism or anti-Jewish would also be correct terms. No other Semitic peoples are included within the usage of the term in this book. In fact, the term <u>anti-Semitism</u> was not developed until the 19th century as will be further discussed in chapter ten. Therefore, no ancient use of the term existed. Nonetheless, anti-Semitism appears to be understood by most moderns in the form I shall be using it throughout this work.

CHAPTER II

ONE JEWISH FAMILY

I am an American born Jew of European descent. The Gentile Christian world has always been interested in the Jewish people but not always interested in their well-being. My father came to Christian America between the pogroms[1] of Catholic Hungary and the Nazis of Germany, birthplace of the Protestant Reformation. My maternal grandfather left Lithuania on foot and literally walked across Europe at the age of fifteen to escape conscription into the Czar's army, which would have been followed by his forced conversion to the Russian Orthodox religion. At that time, Russia, also a Christian nation, had been populated by Orthodox Christians for over 900 years.

---

[1] Pogroms were organized beatings, attacks, and/or massacres of Jews. Generally, these were sanctioned by the government.

DOES JACOB'S TROUBLE WEAR A CROSS?

Shortly thereafter, Russia "boasted 54,457 churches."[5] They could not, however, boast about their treatment of the Jews. In 1908 my Grandmother was put on a boat from Russia with a note pinned to her coat. She was eight years old and alone. She carried with her two rubles, a salami, and a loaf of pumpernickel bread. This was all she had when she came to live with her father. Her aunt, who had cared for her after her mother's death, had also intended to come to America with her. Unfortunately, she had only saved enough for one ticket. Before she could scrape together enough for her own later passage, she was raped and killed in another pogrom.

As might be discerned, Christianity has made a lasting impression on at least one Jewish family. Obviously, many people in so-called Christian nations are not themselves Christian. The victims of violent bigotry are not obliged to check their persecutor's denominational pedigree, nor do they concern themselves with the doctrinal perversions of Scripture employed to rationalize the sin of anti-Semitism. When bigots wear the cross, it serves to devalue the one who bore the cross in the eyes of the victim. Misplaced religious zeal does not mitigate pain. Sadly, the truth of the parable of Jesus is well understood

---

[5] Bradley Nassif, <u>Moody Monthly</u>, "From Kiev to the Kremlin," (Moody Bible Institute, Chicago, IL, Volume 88, Number 10, June, 1988), p. 23.

by Jews who have experienced the wrong side of "Christian love and zeal" in every generation. "You will know them by their fruits. Do men gather grapes from thornbushes or figs of thistles? Even so, every good tree bears good fruit, but a bad tree bears bad fruit" (Matthew 7: 16-17). Centuries of rotten fruit have been tasted by Jewish people who have struggled to survive Gentile persecution. Some of these Gentiles may have been misguided Christians. Others were more likely Christian in name alone. Truly, they all look alike from the victim's side of hatred.

For my predecessors, it was a long, difficult trip to their promised land. If Christians are called to be ambassadors of Christ, Christ has been poorly represented everywhere our family tried to live. Our family began the exodus to America nearly ninety years ago. The American Gentile evangelization efforts have not been successful in provoking this Jewish family to jealousy as expected by the Apostle Paul (Romans 11:11). Rather, the experiences of this single family (undoubtedly not a unique example) have had a detrimental impact. During the last ninety years, we have remained unconvinced that Gentile Christianity offers true salvation. Further, we disbelieve that the need for salvation exists as represented by the Gentile Christian Church. Additionally, modern Christianity has been discredited as a reliable example of moral excellence. Lastly, and my deepest concern, biblical Christianity has been ignored by my family because of the horrible victimization displayed against Jews throughout Christian history. This is not to say that my relatives dislike Gentile Christians. It simply informs Gentile Christians that they have not expressed enough Christian love to merit serious consideration as an alternative or necessary faith. To my knowledge, within my family, I am the only Christian, [6] and I did not come to Christ due to any personal contact with a Christian. Not realizing it was a Christian work, I read a book[7] that related to issues of personal concern. The book included many Scripture verses and God's Word does not return void (Isaiah 55:11). I decided to believe that Jesus truly was the Messiah spoken of in the Hebrew Bible. I am convinced that the Holy Spirit came upon me and convicted me of my sins. I was quite uncomfortable when I was told that I had "converted" to Christianity. <u>Jesus loved me, but what did that have to do with Christianity?</u> I had not experienced Christian love from people who called

---

[6] To clarify, this writer does have one female cousin who married a Gentile Christian and later took on his religion.

[7] Hal Lindsey, *The Late Great Planet Earth*, (Zondervan Publishing, Grand Rapids, MI, 1970).
I read Mr. Lindsey's book twenty-two years ago. Today I do not agree with all of his doctrinal conclusions. Thankfully, the Christian faith provides room for disagreement on certain nonessentials. Regardless of those disagreements, I am highly grateful to him for his efforts.

themselves Christians. I had not actually witnessed long-term Christian commitment. Really, it was quite confusing.

I will always be forced to deal with words spoken to me by my Jewish parents. They reminded me that I was a traitor. They asked to legally change my name. I was forced to deal with their silence because for several years they refused to speak to me. In all of this, God never permitted me to doubt their love. I realized that their actions were not based upon hatred. They were merely reacting to their pain. Perhaps from their perspective the Gentile Christian Church had simply inflicted one more punishment on the Jewish people. My family could not understand that God was working in my life. They were convinced that I was proselytized by a fast-talking salesmen of the gospel. Painfully, they struggled to understand how I could have aligned myself with people who had hated, persecuted, tortured, and killed Jewish people for centuries. I informed my parents that those people were not <u>really</u> Christians. They merely called themselves Christians. I comforted myself with the presumptive belief that they must have been violent infidels who manipulated society through their hatred, falsely calling themselves Christians.

Today I am grievously forced to report that history supports the view of my parents. This project is my effort to understand the hatred within my own Christian heritage. I cannot change the past but I do have certain responsibilities for the future. I can promote the truth about Christian history. I can also promote the truth about the wondrous love of God revealed to us in Jesus. Further, I can expose the sin of Christian anti-Semitism and remind my readers that Christianity was birthed in and is a form of Judaism. I must emphasize that Jesus was an observant Jew who never disposed of His heritage. Therefore, neither will I. I am a Jew, my children are Jews, and my prayer is that their children will always know and appreciate that heritage.

That summarizes my personal history through which I have been motivated to engage myself in this research. One's search for truth can never be completely without bias. Truth however, when discovered, offsets the influence to which bias lays claim. My father, Art Weiss, was once a poor, humble, Hungarian-Jewish immigrant. Though he was forced to drop out of school in the fifth grade, the following research will prove that he had a clearer understanding of certain aspects of Church history than his saddened, Bible-reading, educated son.

This Truth Must Startle

The Church has a very sinful and hideous historical record which I intend to present for your examination. When the anti-Semitic behavior of the Church is revealed, I believe it will be so startling that all who recognize the error will work to prohibit its reoccurences. I am sorry that I defended this history of hatred. This effort to report certain errors of the past is a humble attempt to hold up a mirror for our reflection while I make restitution for my own prior ignorance and pride. Many have apparently forgotten, others simply never realized the awful truth. I fit into the camp of the latter. I must ask, what is your position on the matter? Do you know the history of Christian anti-Semitism? Will you tolerate it in the future?

Bal Shem Tov, the illustrious founder of the Hasidic movement within Judaism, is credited with having counseled his loyal students that "memory is the key to redemption."[8] It is hoped that this research will sound a clarion call to remember the errors of our past thereby insuring faith and good deeds in our future.

The feelings, facts, and logic that will follow in this endeavor of reason are intended to persuade Gentile Christians to walk circumspectly in their attitudes toward God's chosen people. It is not necessary to enjoy this information; what is necessary is to consider its accuracy. I can only hope that Gentile Christians will seek truth and repentance as they recognize some sense of corporate responsibility. My faith stands on the knowledge that God

---

[8] Eli Faber, *A Time For Planting, The First Migration 1654-1820,* (The Johns Hopkins University Press, Baltimore, 1992), p. XI.

is love and we are to be like Him. God has called Jews and Gentiles to enter into a personal relationship with Him. We are the new creatures which God crcatcd in Christ to show Himself to the world. Unity is a requirement, not an option. "That they all may be one, as You, Father, are in Me, and I in You; that they also may be one in Us, that the world may believe that You sent Me" (John 17:21).

CHAPTER III

THE APPLE OF GOD'S EYE

"Crucify him! Yes, kill him! He deserves to die!"
The Jewish mob scene became ugly. They relentlessly
pursued their enemy until in their victory, Jesus suffered his
ultimate humiliation and defeat. In retrospect, it is
painfully obvious; at the hands of an enraged, rushing
swarm of God's children, God's child was brutally
murdered! Oh, everyone knows they did not get their
hands dirty. No, they were sadistically bent on infecting
the disinterested Roman prefect of Judaea, Pontius Pilate.
The shrewd Roman was careful not to get his hands dirty
either, or, if he did, he symbolically washed away the guilt.
This dramatic point of no return in the traditional Passion
Play is depicted in Churches around the world to remind
believers everywhere of the scene preceding the crucifixion
of Jesus Christ, the rejected Jewish Messiah. This writer is
Jewish and accepts the concept that Jesus is the Messiah.
Thus, it is inappropriate to seriously propose that Jesus has
been rejected by the Jews. Since a Jew has accepted Jesus,

proof exists that not all Jewish people have rejected Him. Assuredly, this does not represent a unique, nor primal example of a Jew who believes in Jesus, as many earlier and superior specimens will be discussed.

Depreciating the Chosen People

God has invested Himself in the Jewish people. He did so to such an extent that the Christian Church has no alternative but to reach out to the Jewish people in love, as children of the same God. Documentation will be presented showing how anti-Semitic behavior has been historically propagated by the Christian Church. Although contrary to some evangelicals' view of U.S. history, American Christian culture has not been birthed with a freedom of religion. Rather, it has been charged with subtle forms of, as well as overt, anti-Semitic beliefs. Heinous abuses have been suffered by the Jewish people as a result of erroneous views supported by the Church. This has led to the depreciation of the Jewish people, God's chosen people.

The Jewish people were the original object of His Passion.[9] Unfortunately, the Christian legacy left in the

---

[9] No intent exists to decrease the value that God has placed on the non-Jewish world. The life of Jesus has been sacrificed for Jews and Gentiles alike. Therefore, non-Jewish people are also "the object of His Passion." Scriptural truth is not to be denied. The middle wall of separation between Jews and Gentiles has been broken down. God

hearts of many modern Jewish people is colored by the memories of six million victims of the "Final Solution" wrought by the Nazis during the Holocaust of this century. Even the number "six million" standing alone on a page can evoke painful emotions to a Jew. Inter-religious relations will not approach clear and honest communication standards until the horror of Christian anti-Semitism is understood. This will not occur until the responsibility of the Gentile Christian Church is evaluated by Gentile Christians. Jewish observers already know the truth that has been neglectfully disregarded by some Gentile Christians. Individual guilt is not to be adjudicated and guilt by association is not to be accepted. Nonetheless, knowledge of the past helps bring responsibility for the future. Christian anti-Semitism must be understood, identified, and corrected. Blame is not to be confused with understanding. Guilt is not the goal. The goal is to insure a corrected historical view, with an adjusted attitude leading to genuine Christian love.

The word "depreciate" has been used to describe the devaluation experienced by the Jews in the afterbirth of the

---

sees no racial barriers from His throne. Rather, it is imperative that balance be found where it has been lacking. Every life is sacred, valued, and intensely special to God. The pain of a Jew hurts no more than any other human being. Likewise, the worth of a Jew is no greater than any other life. This effort simply takes to task certain historical problems that may repeat themselves if not effectively addressed in this generation.

DOES JACOB'S TROUBLE WEAR A CROSS?

Church. Jews and Judaism have been greatly depreciated by the Church. A profound thinker of the second century named Oneklos, who was a convert to Judaism, has been credited with presenting the world with the Aramaic translation of the Five Books of Moses. He has also been placed alongside another convert to Judaism named Aquilas[10] who provided the religious world with the Greek translation of the Bible. "Both Onkelos and Aquila are spoken of as proselytes and disciples of Rabbi Akiva who died in 135."[11] The significance of Onkelos (Aquila) is that at a time of horrible struggles for Jews living under Roman domination, he and others converted to Judaism. Onkelos (Aquila) was believed to have been closely related to the Emperor Hadrian. A wonderful Talmudic story has developed around his conversion. He was probably a nephew to the Roman ruler. It is said that he approached his powerful uncle seeking advice about commerce.

Hadrian replied, "If you lack money, my treasury is always at your disposal." But Aquila continued, "I want to journey throughout the world and to meet many men; therefore I want your advice as to what merchandise I should

---

[10] Some confusion exists between these fascinating individuals, Onkelos and Aquila. Their names are sometimes used interchangeably.

[11] Philip Birnbaum, *A Book of Jewish Concepts,* (Hebrew Publishing Co., New York, 1964), pp. 664-665.

take." To this Hadrian replied: "If you see merchandise fallen in price, deal in it, for it will surely rise again and you will gain thereby."

As the story goes, Onkelos went to Palestine. There he studied under Rabbi Eliezer ben Hyrcanus and Rabbi Joshua ben Chananiah. This experience led to his conversion to Judaism. When he returned to Hadrian, Onkelos reported that he had learned the Torah and had become a Jew.

Greatly shocked Hadrian exclaimed, "Who permitted you to do so?" Onkelos answered, "You told me to do so. When I asked your advice as to what merchandise I should trade in, you told me to get all merchandise that is depreciated, for it would surely rise in value again. I searched among all nations for a people which had fallen lower than the Jews but I found none. I therefore bethought myself that they are sure to rise to new heights again."[12]

Onkelos was correct. The greatest literature in the history of all the world has been presented to the world by the Jewish people. Moses, King David, King Solomon, along with the entire cast of ancient Jewish prophets have written words enduring the longest run of best-selling reading known to mankind. Their words have been more read and discussed than any other words ever written.

---

[12] Gershom Bader, translated by Solomon Katz, *The Encyclopedia of Talmudic Sages* (Jason Aronson, Inc., Northvale, N.J., 1988), pp. 222-223.

DOES JACOB'S TROUBLE WEAR A CROSS?

Their words were God's words, but God chose the Jewish people to deliver them to the world. The glory of the Jewish people did not fade with the canonization of the Hebrew Bible. Their purpose did not disappear when the ink dried on the scrolls. Truly, their most important work was yet to begin.

God's greatest testimony to the chosenness of the Jewish people is displayed forever in His choice of a young Jewish virgin to carry His royal seed and bear His royal Son Jesus. Jesus had a Jewish mother and God was His father. <u>Since His Son was a Jew, and the mother of His Son was a Jew, and Joseph, the adoptive father was a Jew, it is without question that God chose the Jews.</u>

God has chosen the Jews, and God loves the Jews. These are two important facts which must be considered, understood, and applied within the framework of the future intentions of many Gentile Christians. In the light of Christian history, it would appear that these facts have been overlooked, intentionally ignored, or negligently under emphasized. It has been asked, almost as a proverb, by suffering Jews facing irrational circumstances: "Why couldn't God choose some other people, at least long enough for us to catch our breath?" The Apostle Paul says salvation has come to the world through the Jews. It is time for this same salvation to come to the Jews, particularly, in their times of need.

Stumblingblocks

Many years ago, this writer penned the thought directed toward discontented folks in the Church: "If anyone stands between you and Jesus, they must be closer than you." This is also true of Christian Anti-Semites. Some Jews might woefully acknowledge that Christian behavior often blocks the way to seeking Jesus. When a Christian stands between a Jew and Christ, it is two Jews against one Gentile and no one ever got close to Jesus by blocking the road to His relationships. Christian bigotry is a hindrance to Jewish souls and Jesus draws closest to those who need Him. No justification exists for perverted forms of Christianity which alienate Jews. Poor Christian representation fails to promote a loving Savior and actually promotes a distorted view of Jesus. Jesus was not a Jewish infidel. Jesus was not the enemy of Jewish victims. Christian anti-Semitism ignores that Christ is still a faithful Jew. Christian bigots become a stumblingblock to Jews, and to the Jewish Savior. Sometimes the infidels are inside the Church keeping the lost from entering.

Jesus came for the lost sheep of the House of Israel. Gentile representatives have no right to change or deny that goal of the Savior. Early Jewish believers successfully overcame their bias against Gentile believers when they identified the truth that Jews and non-Jews alike were to be offered hope in Christ. This fact was new and innovative to the Jewish Church during the early days of the Christian

DOES JACOB'S TROUBLE WEAR A CROSS?

Era. Revolutionary news had arrived when Paul informed the Jewish Christians that God "had opened the door of faith to the Gentiles" (Acts 14:27). Some Jewish Christians were shaken by this revelation and it caused "no small dissension and dispute with them" (Acts 15:2). They had serious doubts about the validity of the idea that God would allow Gentiles into a relationship previously limited to Jewish participants who upheld Jewish standards. The translation of Acts 15:2 by E.V. Rieu suggests a very serious tone, "Paul and Barnabas vigorously opposed them and contested their doctrine."[13] Paul vehemently disagreed with the conclusions of the Jewish Christians from Jerusalem who had insisted upon Gentile circumcision. Jointly, they determined that the matter should be settled by Jewish Christian leaders in Jerusalem.

In spite of the tensions created by the dispensation of grace to the Gentiles, the Jewish Church leaders in Jerusalem were sensitive. They did not hinder the completion of the worthy goal proclaimed by the Good Shepherd. Matthew Henry's Commentary offers an insightful view of the debate held by the Jerusalem Council.

> We have here a council called on this occasion *(v. 6): The apostles and presbyters came together, to consider of this matter.* They

---

[13] Curtis Vaughan, *The Bible From 26 Translations,* (Baker Book House, Grand Rapids, Michigan, 1988), p. 2173.

did not give their judgment rashly. . . . Though they were clear concerning it in their own minds, yet they would take time to consider it, and to hear what might be said by the adverse party. . . . When both sides had been heard, *Peter rose up.* He put them in mind of the commission he had some time ago *to preach the gospel to the Gentiles. You know that from the beginning of the days* of the gospel *God made choice* of one to preach the gospel to the Gentiles, and I was the person chosen, *that the Gentiles by my mouth should hear the word, and believe, v. 7.* Everybody rejoiced that *God had granted to the Gentiles repentance unto life,* and nobody said a word of circumcising them.[14]

Light to the Gentiles

They understood Jesus had come to bring salvation to Jews and Gentiles. This goal spoken by the ancient prophets told of hope for the world. The subject of one messianic text proclaimed that there would be "a light to the Gentiles, That You should be My salvation to the ends of the earth" (Isaiah 49:6b NKJV). This was gloriously fulfilled in the New Testament when Jesus opened the door of salvation which had previously been closed to the Gentiles. Jesus revealed His marvelous intentions when He told His disciples, "I lay down my life for the sheep. And

---

[14] Matthew Henry, *Commentary on the Whole Bible,* (Zondervan Publishing House, Grand Rapids, Michigan, 1960), p. 1694.

other sheep I have, which are not of this fold" (John 10:15b-16a). Earlier in the same chapter, Jesus had identified Himself as the "door of the sheep." He passionately announced to His Jewish audience, "I am the door. If anyone enters by Me, he will be saved" (John 10:9). Jesus did not leave the key in the door permitting future newcoming Gentile converts the option of locking out the Jews. <u>Yet some have seemingly "dead-bolted" the door to salvation from inside the Church</u>. Generations of Jewish people have been eternally alienated because of Christians who have chosen to ignore or perpetuate Christian anti-Semitism.

God has promised the Jews that His love for them will never end. God loves the Jewish people and His Church should not do less. The Church should exemplify God's love, yet too often it has portrayed misguided hatred and religious intolerance of the worst form.

CHAPTER IV

SIX MILLION--MORE THAN A NUMBER

The Gentile Church has not loved enough Jews, nor have they loved Jews enough. The Jewish people have endured much at the hands of "god-fearing" people who did not fear God enough. Tolerating or harboring attitudes of bigotry and hatred is presuming on God's willingness to forgive. Hatred and atrocities committed against Jews have not been ignored by God. As in Dante's Inferno, Hell is acquainted with the baptized.[15] Many Gentile Christians have perpetrated acts of anti-Semitic hatred that would qualify for the deepest recesses of Dante's Inferno. The question to those Christians becomes, "How to climb out?" Hatred carries with it responsibility and violence leaves an estate. Six million souls have recently been sacrificed to

---

[15] In Dante's *Divine Comedy*, Hell is no stranger to Christians who have intentionally hurt others. Actually, special punishments were prepared for certain church leaders. Of course, Dante's work is fictional, right?

35

that violence. They have increased the flame's intensity and the estate guarantees that it will be a long hard climb out.

<u>Cheap Grace</u>

Hidden in the open arms of Christianity are pretenders serving other gods. Dietrich Bonhoeffer lived through most of the Nazi Holocaust and died a Christian martyr a few days prior to the allied liberation. This Christian saint suffered and died with the Jewish people. He was unwilling to disregard the Jewish cries which the Church wantonly ignored . Bonhoeffer coined the term "cheap grace" as a definitive response to the sinful negligence of the Church. Of the Church he wrote,

> We justified the world, and condemned as heretics those who tried to follow Christ. The result was that a nation became Christian and Lutheran, but at the cost of true discipleship. The price it was called upon to pay was all too cheap. Cheap grace had won the day. . . . The price we are having to pay to-day in the shape of the collapse of the organized Church is only the inevitable consequence of our policy of making grace available to all at too low a cost.[16]

---

[16] Dietrich Bonhoeffer, *The Cost of Discipleship*, (Macmillan Publishing Company, New York, 1963), pp. 58-59.

It would be wrong to suggest that Hitler was a Christian, and as such, Christians killed six million Jews. Bonhoeffer cast a more realistic shadow on the darkness of those days.

> We gave away the word and sacrament wholesale, we baptized, confirmed, and absolved a whole nation unasked and without condition . . . We poured forth unending streams of grace. But the call to follow Jesus in the narrow way was hardly ever heard. . . . With us it has been abundantly proved that the sins of the fathers are visited upon the children unto the third and fourth generations. Cheap grace has turned out to be utterly merciless to our Evangelical Church. This cheap grace has been no less disastrous to our own spiritual lives. Instead of opening up the way to Christ, it has closed it.[17]

Bonhoeffer was horrifyingly accurate about the responsibility of the Church in Germany. A vivid picture is required to gain attention in this effort to win renewed advocacy for the Jewish people. Call to remembrance the persecuted Jews in Germany. Think about violent anti-Semitic zeal. Imagine burned temples and tortured rabbis. See weeping elderly Jewish grandparents. Hear them screaming as their children and children's children are scattered while their houses are ransacked and destroyed. Try to feel the scorching heat emitted from bonfires of

---

[17] Ibid.

DOES JACOB'S TROUBLE WEAR A CROSS?

books piled high on the funeral pyre of God's words.
Envision holy scrolls of the Torah being heaved onto the
implacable, ever-rising flames being sacrificed to gods of
hate. Smell the ash-blackened, sacred parchment skins.
They light the night as smoking, death-ridden fuel for the
fires of bigotry. Who should be tormented in the fire of the
punishment in an Inferno? Listen carefully to these words
of a zealous German:

> What then shall we do with this damned,
> rejected race of Jews? Since they live among us
> and we know about their lying and blasphemy and
> cursing, we cannot tolerate them if we do not
> wish to share in their lies, curses, and blasphemy.
> In this way we cannot quench the inextinguishable
> fire of divine rage . . . Let me give you my honest
> advice.
>
> First, their synagogues or Churches should be
> set on fire, and whatever does not burn up should
> be covered or spread over with dirt so that no one
> may ever be able to see a cinder or stone of it.
> And this ought to be done for the honour of God
> and of Christianity in order that God may see that
> we are Christians, and that we have not wittingly
> tolerated or approved of such public lying, cursing
> and blaspheming of His Son and His Christians. . .
>
> Secondly, their homes should likewise be
> broken down and destroyed. For they perpetuate
> the same things there that they do in their
> synagogues. For the same reason they ought to
> be put under one roof or in a stable, like gypsies.

Thirdly, they should be deprived of their prayer-books and Talmuds in which such idolatry, lies, cursing, and blasphemy are taught.

Fourthly, their rabbis must be forbidden under threat of death to teach any more . . .

Fifthly, passport and traveling privileges must be absolutely forbidden to the Jews. For they have no business in the rural districts, since they are not nobles, nor officials, nor merchants, nor the like . . .

Sixthly, they ought to be stopped from usury. All their cash and valuables of silver and gold ought to be taken from them and put aside for safe keeping. For this reason, as said before, everything that they possess they stole and robbed from us through their usury, for they have no other means of support . . . Such evilly acquired money is cursed, unless, with God's blessing, it is put to some good and necessary use . . .

If however we are afraid that they might harm us personally . . . then let us apply the same cleverness as the other nations, such as France, Spain, Bohemia, etc., and settle with them for that which they have extorted usuriously from us, and after having divided it up fairly let us drive them out of the country for all time. For, as has been said, God's rage is so great against them that they only become worse and worse through mild mercy, and not much better through severe mercy. Therefore away with them . . .[18]

---

[18] William Nicholls, *Christian Antisemitism, A History of Hate,* (Jason Aronson Inc., Northvale, NJ, 1993), pp. 270-271.

DOES JACOB'S TROUBLE WEAR A CROSS?

Horrifying, frightening, enlightening! "At his trial in Nuremberg after the Second World War, Julius Streicher, the notorious Nazi propagandist, editor of the scurrilous antisemitic weekly, *Der Sturmer*, argued that if he should be standing there arraigned on such charges"[19] another famous German should have also been there with him. The author of this plan was not his boss, Adolf Hitler. The author of those despicable words of hatred toward Jews was not even penned by a German Nazi; they were from our revered German hero of the faith, Martin Luther, the father of the Protestant Reformation.

Reformers, Popes and the Talmud

The previous quote from the zealous German, Martin Luther, shows his attitude toward the Jewish people. He actually believed, "And this ought to be done for the honour of God."[20] Martin Luther believed that Christians actually honored God by destroying synagogues, burning Talmuds,[21] and issuing death threats against humble, aged

---

[19] Ibid.

[20] Ibid.

[21] The Talmud represents one of the most significant portions of Jewish knowledge and understanding. It is the compilation of the entire oral law which was composed by Palestinian and Babylonian sages. The two principle sections of the Talmud include the Mishnah, which conveys *halakah* (the law) and the commentaries on

rabbis. With horror and grief it must be reported that similar sentiments have plagued the Jews for many centuries prior to Luther and since. Christian anti-Semitism must be seen for what it is, a horrible sin of hatred!

Luther was not the first Christian leader to maliciously call for the desolation of sacred Jewish writings. Rulers of the Christian Church in various centuries sought to destroy the Talmud.

---

the law, known as the Gemarah. According to scholarly Jewish opinion, "The Talmud is the repository of thousands of years of Jewish wisdom, and the oral law, which is as ancient and significant as the written law (the Torah), finds expression therein." Talmudic writings incorporate the essentials of what is relevant to Jewish learning. "It is a conglomerate of law, legend, and philosophy, a blend of unique logic and shrewd pragmatism, of history and science, anecdotes and humor. It is a collection of paradoxes: its framework is orderly and logical, every word and term subjected to meticulous editing, completed centuries after the actual work of composition came to an end." The rigorous demands of disciplined learning is a religious duty to the truly committed practitioner of Orthodox Judaism. "The Talmud is the embodiment of the great concept of *mitzvat talmud Torah*--the positive religious duty of studying Torah, of acquiring learning and wisdom, study which is its own end and reward." An accepted view among religious Jews toward the study of Talmud is best explained by one of the devoted students of the Talmud. "A certain Talmudic sage who has left us nothing but his name and this one dictum had this to say on the subject: 'Turn it and turn it again, for everything is contained in the Torah. Regard it and grow old in it and never abandon it, for there is no greater virtue.'" This information comes from Adin Steinsaltz, *The Essential Talmud*, (Jason Aronson, Northvale, New Jersey, 1992) pages 4-5.

This anti-talmudic campaign and the various decrees of the popes reached their height when. . . Pope Gregory IX ordered the burning of copies of the Talmud in Paris in 1240. Similar decrees were issued several times in the course of the thirteenth century, on one occasion by Pope Clement IV in 1264, and thousands of copies were consigned to the flames. The Jews regarded the destruction of the Talmud as an almost unparalleled national catastrophe.[22]

In 1509 Johannes Pfefferkorn worked to convince the guides of the church "to burn the Talmud in all countries under the rule of Charles V."[23] Fortunately this effort was unsuccessful. Unfortunately, by 1553 Pope Julius III successfully had tens of thousands of copies of the sacred Talmud burned. In other situations, when church leaders could not get support to burn the Talmud, they worked to censor it. These efforts resulted in many textual perversions to satisfy the Church's need to try to control the thinking and teaching of the Jews. The value of understanding the devastation felt by Jews of various time periods over the burning, desecration, or perversion of their books (which happened on many occasions in history) is provided to express the high value placed on learning,

---

[22] Adin Steinsaltz, *The Essential Talmud*, (Jason Aronson, Northvale, New Jersey, 1992), pp. 82-83.

[23] Ibid.

and the indescribable loss felt when Christians tried to destroy the Jewish knowledge base. As sages disappeared in history, only their teachings remained to guide subsequent generations into the truths the sages had discovered. Jewish life has been grounded in these ideas. Those intent on destroying the Jewish people have historically attacked their methods of storing and conveying such ideas.

Virulent anti-Semitism has infected the roots of the Church. Martin Luther is a true hero of the faith. His tireless efforts to bring truth to the saints were worthy of all the praise heaped upon him over the centuries. His commitment to grace, faith, and the sanctity of Scripture are momentous. He wrote, *"unum, simplicem, germanum, et certum sensum literalum"* meaning "Each passage has one clear, definite, and true sense of its own. All others are but doubtful and uncertain opinions."[24] This revelation from Luther was both orthodox and brilliant. Luther's method of Scripture interpretation has been helpful to Evangelical Christianity. Still, he hated the Jewish people. He was frustrated with their unwillingness to accept Christ. This frustration apparently turned into bitterness and hatred. Luther's error has been discussed by Hal Lindsey in

---

[24] F. W. Farrar, *History of Interpretation,* (New York: E. P. Dutton, 1886) pp. 325-30, as quoted by J. Dwight Pentecost, *Things To Come,* (Zondervan Publishing House, Grand Rapids, Michigan,1969), p.28.

DOES JACOB'S TROUBLE WEAR A CROSS?

a fine work exposing sickening doctrinal deviations that have led to the ongoing alienation of Jews by misguided Christians.

The fact that such a great man of faith and the Scriptures as Luther could be seduced by Satan to write such a monstrous thing proves two things:

First, the anti-Jewish propaganda within the Church and society in general was virulently latent and thoroughly embedded in the culture.[25]

Second, the original false interpretation of prophecy, which Luther retained from Augustine, was a powerful blinding force that kept even the great reformer, who was an otherwise brilliant and literal interpreter of the Scriptures, from grasping what God's Word literally and unconditionally taught: that the Jews are still His elect people with a definite future in His plan. It also kept him from seeing an oft repeated Biblical lesson: that even though God Himself disciplines Israel, woe

---

[25] This fact was permanently driven home to this writer recently while speaking with Dr. Jeffrey Seif, the head of the Jewish Studies Department at Christ For The Nations Institute. Dr. Seif commented on this fact. He said that Martin Luther did not use any ingenuity in deciding to invoke his hateful words against the Jewish people. In fact, he was simply a product of his environment. This in no wise justifies his attitude or behavior. It merely helps to explain it. Actually, as Dr. Seif stated it, Martin Luther's sin consisted of ignoring this horrible error which was prevalent in Luther's world. In effect, he missed an opportunity to nail a few more additional pages onto the famous Wittenberg Door. If he had, the history of the Jews of Europe might have been completely different.

to the man or nation who mistreats them. History
is strewn with the wreckage of former great
leaders and nations who treated the Israelites
unjustly.[26]

---

[26] Hal Lindsey, *The Road To Holocaust*, (Bantam Books, New
York, New York, 1989), p. 24. Mr. Lindsey should be heartily
commended for his effort. His text is clearly offered from the heart of
a non-Jewish believer in Jesus who has identified the correct posture
to maintain toward God's people. He chooses to love and protect
through teaching valuable information to help the Church know their
past. He does this with propriety and love to aid their genuine move
toward God's future call on His Church. On Page 25 of his text, Mr.
Lindsey defined his purpose for the book as follows: "One of the
main reasons I write this book is to seek to prevent Christians from
once again contributing to this same kind of tragedy (even though it
may be through ignorance). I believe we are witnessing a growing
revival of the same false interpretation of prophecy that in the past
led to such tragedy for so many centuries by a movement that calls
itself either Reconstructionism, Dominionism and/or Kingdom Now."
(Please do not confuse this with the branch of Judaism known as
Reconstructionist.)

CHAPTER V

CHILDREN OF ISRAEL--CHILDREN OF GOD

God loves the Children of Israel. These include all of the descendants who trace their lineage back through the patriarchs Abraham, Isaac, and Jacob. Abraham was identified by James as "the friend of God" (James 2:23). Israel, previously known as Jacob, holds a unique place in God's sight.

> For the portion of the LORD is his people,
> Jacob the lot of His inheritance. He found him in
> a desert land, And in the waste, a howling
> wilderness; He compassed him about, He cared
> for him, He kept him as the apple of His eye
> (Deuteronomy 32:9-10).

Unlike God, Gentile Christians have not viewed the Children of Israel as the apple of their eye. Apparently they have not seen the descendants of Jacob through God's eyes. God loves the Jews.

Suffering At The Hand Of God

God often chose to judge or punish His people. Examples abound in their wilderness experiences described in the writings of Moses, their frustrated desert leader. Tests, failures, and chastisements continued throughout the periods of disobedience under Joshua and the Judges of Israel. Further afflictions came during the days of glory when kings reigned in the unified nation of Israel. Even when God was worshipped in Solomon's Temple, disobedience inevitably brought punishment by God. Yet, God's attitude toward His people's future remained constant. Suffering was always temporary, the promises were always eternal.

Warnings from the Hebrew prophets were intended to prepare God's wayward sons and daughters. It is certain that God sent judgment as punishment for disobedience. Nevertheless, the dutiful prophets also reminded the Children of Israel that God's hand of chastening would eventually bring redemption to His people.

Their disobedience led to being wrenched from their homeland or placed into slavery on more than one occasion. The Children of Israel were oppressed by God's chosen adversaries. With much pain they were adjusted by God to meet God. God never changed to meet them.

Throughout millennia of imposed struggles <u>the Jews remained firmly embedded in an unmovable place deep within the heart of God</u>: "Surely, he that toucheth you toucheth the apple of his eye" (Zechariah 2:12).[27]

The adversaries chosen by God to chastise His children were often wicked, pagan, violent vessels fitted for destruction. Ultimately, the adversaries were then destroyed. In effect, Israel's enemies only served a temporary purpose. Once their jobs were done, their own wickedness brought their own destruction.

God judged Israel's sinful idolatry in 722 BCE when the northern kingdom of Israel was brutally conquered by the Assyrian army. Nahum prophesied that the Assyrians would fall when God brought judgment to Israel's oppressor. In 612 BCE, Ninevah, the Assyrian capital, was conquered as predicted. The rise of the Babylonian empire brought judgment upon the southern kingdom of Judah in 586 BCE. After the Babylonians had served God's purposes in the seventy-year Jewish exile, the Babylonians were deposed. Persia conquered Babylon in 539 BCE after Daniel's famous interpretation of the handwriting on the wall (Daniel 5:25). Wicked empires replaced other wicked empires until God's judgment on His chosen people was

---

[27] For readers more familiar with Christian Bibles, this verse is worded almost identically, however, in Christian Bibles it is found at verse 8 due to a variance in the chapter breaks of the Hebrew Bible.

DOES JACOB'S TROUBLE WEAR A CROSS?

completed and the wicked empires earned their own judgment. The blessings of God never lasted on the enemies of the Children of Israel.

Enemies In Error

This characterization of Israel's enemies is not flattering. Christian anti-Semites must reckon with the company they join if they mistakenly believe they serve God in chastising a rebellious race. In truth, they shift from sharing in God's eternal purpose to serving in a very temporary position. God will never abandon the Children of Israel, therefore, Zechariah's words should also temper the attitudes of every enemy of the Jews. In the end, they will find that they hurt God when they hurt those whom He loves. When they attack God's chosen people, they attack the "apple of His eye."

Christian anti-Semites do not love the Jewish people. This has resulted in the presentation of an image of Christ who does not love the Jewish people. Some Gentile Christians have acted as though Jesus forgives everyone except the Jews. The message heard loud and clear by the Jews has been that "they killed Christ and He is going to pay them back." J. B. Phillips translation of the New Testament describes in chapter 10 of The Letter to the Jewish Christians (Hebrews), that God alone takes full responsibility for issuing punishment.

The man who showed contempt for Moses'
Law died without hope of appeal on the evidence
of two or three witnesses. How much more
dreadful a punishment will he be thought to
deserve who has poured scorn on the Son of God
. . . Vengeance belongeth unto me, I will
recompense. And again: The Lord shall judge his
people."[28]

The Hebrew Bible provides ample evidence that His judgment was often meted out by pagan enemies or oppressors. The punishments were thorough, painful, and effective. One example of the effectiveness can be seen in the fact that before their exile in 586 BCE, idolatry had plagued Jewish existence for many centuries. In contradistinction, post-exilic Israel had no significant problem with idolatry. The depth of the scourging experienced in the Babylonian captivity was sufficient to teach the lesson that God wanted taught to His children. He was their God, and they were to worship no other gods. Idolatry became abhorrent to the Children of Israel. This hatred of idolatry, combined with the knowledge of the punishment that idolatry brings, has led to the eradication of that strain of national sin within God's people. Even modern Judaism considers that form of disobedience to be

---

[28] J. B. Phillips, *The New Testament in Modern English*, (Macmillan Publishing Co., Inc., New York, 1977) p. 469.

loathsome.[29] Idolatry is so distasteful to some Jews that the icons of Catholicism and Greek or Russian Orthodoxy appear to be an abomination.

At various points in Church history, well-meaning Gentile Christians have determined that the Jews deserved punishment for their role in the death of Jesus. Many Jews have been killed as infidels as part of Christian service. Apparently, some Christians independently determined that God was too slow and merciful. Instead of waiting for God to repay in His own time, religious vigilantes willingly offered their hands to punish Jews. Since the time when the mantle of Church leadership and membership passed into Gentile Christian hands, many Jews have suffered in the name of Christ. This should not be forgotten. Gentile Christians should be aware of their heritage of error toward God's chosen people.

God always sent the Hebrew prophets to warn the Children of Israel when their actions were drawing God's judgment. The Hebrew prophets are now silent. The canon of Scripture is closed. Jeremiah, Isaiah, Zephaniah, Habakkuk, Amos, and other prophets of doom, have

---

[29] This lesson was learned the hard way. It will never be forgotten. Potentially, that eschatology which suggests that the Jews of the endtimes will identify the error of the Antichrist when they are called upon to worship something other than God refers back to the understanding that idolatry brings judgment from God.

finished writing. The majority of their messages on Israel's judgment have been fulfilled. The remaining prophecies now seem to focus on the regathering of Israel, not its condemnation. Unlike the Assyrians, Babylonians, and other ordained adversaries of the ancient Jews, Christians hold no writ disposing them to carry out God's supposed punishment against modern Jews. Perhaps Christians of the Dark Ages and Middle Ages did not have sufficient information or access to Scripture to make better choices in their relationships with their Jewish neighbors. Modern Christians cannot use that argument. Eschatology suggests that prior to the return of Jesus an evil world system will yet cruelly dominate and destroy. Certainly believing Christians do not wish to participate in that divine program of vengeance. The remaining biblical alternative is to share Christian love and hope in preparation for the messianic age which Christians believe will follow the endtime judgment.

The Holy Spirit is certainly capable of speaking to modern men and women. God's still, small voice can yet be heard by those who listen and modern "prophets" do speak words of life to God's Church. Still, no new prophecies will be added to the Bible. God wrote the last chapter exactly as He desired. Harsh, new "prophecies" should be carefully evaluated before being accepted. Today's "prophets" should be very cautious about delivering zealous words of condemnation.

DOES JACOB'S TROUBLE WEAR A CROSS?

One famous verse used to justify harsh words from modern "prophets" is "Surely the Lord God will do nothing, but he revealeth his secret unto his servants, the prophets" (Amos 3:7 KJV). Modern "prophets" should not act as though this verse gives them license to preach judgment and condemnation. In total, Amos tells a different story.

> Hear this word that the Lord hath spoken against you, O children of Israel, against the whole family which I brought up from the land of Egypt, saying, ***You only have I known of all the families of the earth: therefore I will punish you for all your iniquities.*** Can two walk together, except they be agreed? Will a lion roar in the forest, when he hath no prey? Will a young lion cry out of his den, if he have taken nothing? Can a bird fall in a snare upon the earth, where no gin (trap) is for him? Shall one take up a snare from the earth, and have taken nothing at all? Shall a trumpet be blown in the city, and the people not be afraid? ***Shall there be evil in a city, and the Lord hath not done it?*** Surely the Lord God will do nothing, but he revealeth his secret unto his servants, the prophets. The lion hath roared, who will not fear? The Lord God hath spoken, who can but prophesy? Publish in the palaces at Ashdod, and in the palaces in the land of Egypt, and say, Assemble yourselves upon the mountains of Samaria, and behold the great tumults in the midst thereof, and the oppressed in the midst therof. For they know not to do right, saith the Lord, who store up violence and robbery

in their palaces. ***Therefore thus saith the Lord God; An adversary there shall be*** even round about the land; and he shall bring down thy strength from thee, and thy palaces shall be spoiled (italics mine, Amos 3:1-11 KJV).

God gave a mandate to that adversary. God brought "evil" events upon His children to turn them from their course of wickedness in the days of Amos (approximately 760 BCE). Shortly thereafter the destruction which Amos foretold came to pass. But the hatred and destruction poured out on the Jewish people since the time of Christ by Christians carries no mandate from God. Those Christians disregard, or steal for themselves, the balance of the promises God made to His children.

Amos did not end his message declaring the permanent destruction of the Jewish people. The specific punishment decreed by God to fall on Israel and Judah was temporary and corrective in nature. In God's economy, blessings eventually follow obedience, while judgment eventually follows disobedience. The end of Amos' message informs the reader,

Behold, the eyes of the Lord GOD Are upon the sinful kingdom, And I will destroy it from off the face of the earth; ***Saving that I will not utterly destroy the house of Jacob, Saith the LORD***. For, lo, I will command, and I will sift the house of Israel among all the nations, Like as corn is sifted in a sieve, Yet shall not the least grain fall upon the earth. All the sinners of My people shall die by the sword, That say: "The evil shall not overtake nor confront us." In that day will I raise up The tabernacle of David that is fallen, And close up the breaches thereof, And I will raise up his ruins, And I will build it as in the days of old; That they may possess the remnant of Edom, ***And all the nations*** ("Gentiles" NKJV), ***upon whom My name is called,*** Saith the LORD that doeth this. . . . And I will turn the captivity of My people Israel, And they shall build the waste cities, and inhabit them . . . And I will plant them upon their land, ***And they shall no more be plucked up Out of their land which I have given them***, Saith the LORD thy God. (italics mine, Amos 9: 8-12, 14a, 15).

The Children of Israel experienced God's judgment, but Amos assures them that they will also experience God's restoration. Both judgment and restoration are God's prerogatives. The Church has experienced and has been called to display God's love.

This research draws the history of Christianity into focus. In so doing, it calls the future of Christianity into question. The Children of Israel will be restored. God's promise is secure. Christian love is the most effective tool available to the Church if they are to participate in God's restorative process.

CHAPTER VI

CHILDREN OF GOD, VICTIMS OF ZEAL

The Church can show no "warrant" which ordains them to minister violent anti-Semitic behavior. Regardless, some Christians have carved a scar on the history of Jewish-Christian relations that will not be easily overlooked, though some would seek to try.

The Wrong Crusade

The publisher of <u>Christianity Today</u>, a very credible, well-respected periodical recently printed a journal discussing the Crusades. Mark Galli, the Associate Editor, issued these deplorable comments in "From the Editor" including the following flawed justification for the Crusades:

> But the crusaders were real Christians. They deplored their sins. They longed for forgiveness. They loved fellow Christians in the East. They yearned to do something noble and lasting for their Lord. They prayed and fasted before battles and praised God after victories. Their devotion and courage make ours look juvenile.

> So much of what they did was wrong. Yes, and all have sinned and fallen short of the glory of God. So there's little point in becoming judgmental.[30]

This sounds like something which might be acceptable had the church deacon taken the pastor's assigned parking place, or failed to tithe on his bingo winnings, but Mr. Galli's logic fails in the light of the degradation and horrifying sinful violence perpetrated on generations of suffering human beings in the name of Christ. According to Mr. Galli's own later comments, the Crusades lasted from 1096 through the sixteenth century. The same journal reported,

> When Pope Urban II rallied Christians, he offered an extraordinary reward to those who set out to liberate the land of the Savior's birth: "All who die by the way, whether by land or by sea, or in battle against pagans, shall have immediate remission of sins."[31]

The decree was effective in enlisting soldiers for the battle, but one doubts that forgiveness was immediate or complete. The Pope was extremely generous with the grace of God and the blood of Christ, and the crusaders were generous with the blood of Jews.

---

[30] Kevin A. Miller, Editor, "The Crusades," <u>Christian History</u>, Issue 90, Volume XII, Number 4, 1993, p. 6.

[31] Ibid., p. 19.

Jews in various German towns were "unwillingly forced into baptism" or slaughtered by unruly crusaders in 1096. Here, rather than be converted or killed, the Jews in Worms commit suicide. A Christian chronicler wrote, "It is a sin even to tell how mothers pierced and cut throats of their nursing babes." Before the pogroms ended, some 5,000 Jews had been killed.[32]

There were so many rapes perpetrated against Jewish women during ancient Christian persecutions that the determining factor of the Jewish bloodline had to be changed from the paternal to the maternal line. This commentary, although emotional, betrays the most accurate perception of centuries of Jewish victimization. During the Crusades, Christian leaders took oaths committing themselves to remain in the country until they "killed a Jew with their own hands." Many were deluded by the thought that "killing a Jew would secure atonement for one's sins."[33] The killer instinct seemed to be insatiable, and Jews were not the only victims.

During the eleventh and twelfth centuries, crusading fervor broke out into savage persecutions of Jews. Although some bishops tried to stop them, Christians in the First Crusade slaughtered entire villages of Jews along the Rhine

---

[32] Ibid., p. 43.

[33] Max L. Margolis, and Alexander Marx, *A History of the Jewish People*, (A Temple Book, Atheneum, New York, 1973). p. 360.

River. In Spain and Portugal, crusade-like wars against the Muslims continued for nearly 800 years. This "perpetual crusade," known as the Reconquest, did not end until 1492 under Isabella and Ferdinand.[34]

Unbelievable as it may seem, <u>Jewish life was much better under the Moslem rule</u>, than under Christian domination.

During the Middle Ages, the Jews of Spain had flourished under Moslem rule, participating in the economic and public life of the country and simultaneously creating a rich Hebraic culture of their own. With the resurgence of the Christians in Spain, who gradually reestablished hegemony from their bases in the northern part of the peninsula and ultimately drove out the Moslems, the tide began to turn against the Jews. In 1391, massacres of Jews erupted across Spain, and thousands of them consequently converted to Christianity, accepting baptism in order to preserve lives.[35]

In any form, anti-Semitism is despicable. In a Christian frame of reference, it is all the more deplorable. The earlier use of Paul's famous words to the Romans "all have sinned," were used by Mr. Galli in an apparent attempt to seek justification for the sins of the Crusaders.

---

[34] Miller, <u>Christian History</u>, p. 3.

[35] Faber, p. 5.

However, even if the Crusaders were Christians, even if they hated their sins, even if they loved other Christians, even if their intentions were noble, even if they fasted and prayed, and even if they praised God, what they did was wrong; what they did was sin; what they did was not glorifying to God, therefore, there is a point in being judgmental. Paul's later question asks, "What shall we say then? Shall we continue in sin, that grace may abound? God forbid" (Romans 6:1-2).

Christians are in sinful error when they do not love God's chosen people. From the twelfth chapter of Genesis to the end of the Bible, it is written to the Jews, by the Jews, for the Jews, and generally about the Jews.[36] This information could rapidly lead a casual reader to conclude that the Church is in error if adherents are permitted to hate those who are the principal subjects of the book.

The journal, Christian History, asks several questions about the Crusades in an interview with Jonathan Riley-Smith. The last question was interesting. "What should we think of the crusaders?" That question should be simple to answer. Although it is understood that noble

---

[36] Obviously, some exceptions exist and certainly, Gentiles are considered in the Bible. They were often used as Israel's adversaries when God wanted to punish the Jews. God offered specific promises to Gentiles that ultimately led to their inclusion in the Jewish Church, and Jewish chosenness, as revealed in the New Testament. The error occurs when Gentiles assume they have replaced the Jews, as opposed to having joined the Jews in their chosenness.

intentions to regain the holy land for the glory of God was at the center of the Church's motives, the answer to "What should we think" seems apparent. Answers such as "appalling," "abhorrent," or even "impossible" are all incorrect based upon Riley-Smith's response. He suggests,

> First, we need to understand that medieval
> crusaders are likely to be our relatives. If you are
> of Western European origin, you have nearly a
> 100-percent chance of being a direct descendant
> of someone who had a link with a crusade. . . .
> were these people trying to express love of God
> and neighbor through crusading? Though I
> cannot condone all of their actions, I have to say
> they were.[37]

More appropriately, universal repentance would seem to be the most appropriate response. The "love of God and neighbor" might be expressed through car-pooling, but never through crusading. Mass murder and blood-thirsty slaughter is hardly the methodology of Jesus. Therefore, it should not be tolerated as the expression of Christian love in any historical setting.

---

[37] Miller, <u>Christian History</u>, p. 45.

CHAPTER VII

HEROES OR SCOUNDRELS, A MATTER OF INTERPRETATION

Several significant personalities in Church history have shaped the trends that led to widespread Christian anti-Semitism. Additionally, a review into the most common methods of interpreting the Bible will be helpful in understanding the wrong turn that has led the Church down that road of anti-Semitism. It will not be difficult to see how the Church slipped in the search for truth and fell on its destructive path of ungodly hatred.

Attitudes of the Church and its perspective toward Judaism changed drastically after the second century. The Gentile Church leaders began to show dislike and disregard for Jews. This was first seen in the writings of Justin Martyr in his *Dialogue With Trypho*. "His text provides a viewing platform from which one may witness the fire that eventually burned and destroyed the original church--

Messianic Judaism."[38] Justin Martyr reveals the attitudes of the Church toward Jews during the middle of the second century. He was questioned by a Jewish teacher. The query dealt with the subject of Jewish conversions. One specific question at issue was whether or not a Jew could be saved if he continued to maintain the Jewish law.

> Justin replied that they would, provided they did not insist on other Christians doing likewise. But he also warned that not all Christians shared his tolerant attitude. The incident reveals that the Church was by this time a predominantly Gentile body.[39]

Since many Jews did not accept Christ during the second and third centuries, the Church chose to regard Jews as a lost, cursed, apostate people without hope. Even their mark of circumcision took on new meaning according to Justin Martyr.

> Circumcision was given to the Jews as a sign of Cain. Thus Justin Martyr wrote in *Dialogue with Trypho* that "Circumcision according to the flesh, which is from Abraham, was given for a sign, that you alone may suffer that which you

---

[38] Jeffrey Seif, *Origin of the Christian Faith,* (JSM Publishing in cooperation with Christ For The Nations Institute, Dallas, TX, 1992), p. 218.

[39] Tim Dowley, Org. Ed., *Eerdman's Handbook to The History of Christianity,* (Wm. B. Eerdmans Publishing Company, Grand Rapids, Michigan, 1988), p. 100.

now justly suffer" . . . As wandering figures--
homeless and reviled by God and man--the Jews
lack any means of salvation.[40]

Hope of the Gentiles--Curse of the Jews

Sometimes creative thinking leads to change.
Sometimes change leads to improvements. At other times,
change leads to depreciation, devaluation, and depravity.

> Martyr's works are invaluable because they
> give us an important perspective on mid-second
> century Christianity. Because Martyr is credited
> with the teaching that Gentiles have replaced the
> Jews in God's economy, we can infer, *ipso facto*,
> that his teaching didn't exist long before his time.
> To date, the theology of the early church fit well
> within the bounds of normative Judaism. In fact,
> the "movement" at first existed as an unpopular
> sect within Judaism.[41]

Jeffrey Seif quotes Elizabeth Livingstone as she sums up
the career of Justin Martyr.

> Though of no great philosophical or literary
> skill, Justin was the first Christian thinker to seek
> to reconcile the claims of faith and reason. His
> 'First Apology' (c. 155) was addressed to the
> Emperor Antonius Pius and his adopted sons. It
> defends Christianity as the only true rational creed

---

[40] Dan Cohn-Sherbok, *The Crucified Jew: Twenty Centuries of Christian Anti-Semitism*, (HarperCollins Publishers, London, 1992), p. 34.

[41] Seif, p. 268.

and contains an account of the contemporary Baptismal ceremonies and Eucharistic belief and practice. The 'Second apology', addressed to the Roman Senate, is concerned to rebut specific charges against the Christians. In his 'Dialogue With Trypho the Jew' Justin develops the identity of the Logos with the God of the Old Testament *and the vocation of the Gentiles to take the place of Israel.*[42]

The relationship between the Jews and the Gentile Church deteriorated very rapidly from that point into an open and legalized form of discrimination by the time of Constantine. Momentum for the spread of Christian anti-Semitism came from new methods of Bible interpretations. Men like Origen were fundamental to the change.

Origen was born in 185 CE to a Christian family in Alexandria. He became a respected teacher and writer who lived as a committed ascetic. He is recognized as one of the early Church leaders whose inventiveness provided significant contributions to Christian history. Sadly, all of his efforts did not lead to a more effective, righteous Church built on biblical principles. His efforts to allegorize Scripture, allowing for three levels of interpretation for

---

[42] Elizabeth Livingstone, *The Concise Oxford Dictionary of the Christian* Church (New York: Oxford University Press, 1987), p. 284, as quoted by Jeffrey Seif, *Origin of the Christian Faith,* (JSM Publishing in cooperation with Christ For The Nations Institute, Dallas, TX, 1992), pp. 267-268.

biblical texts, significantly effected scholars and theologians
for many centuries. He tried to relate his views and ideas
in a fashion that would be understood among the Platonic
philosophical schools of his time. Conservative
Churchmen today would be vexed by his methods.
Without question, Origen was sincere in his efforts, and as
a loyal believer he was responsible for many important
writings of the early Church. These included the *Hexapla*,
which may have been the finest example of biblical
scholarship generated by the early Church.[43]   Origen was
very inluential, but he was also a troubled individual.
Opting for a literal interpretation of Matthew 19:12, he
castrated himself.[44]

Origen's allegorical treatment of God's Word
supported the deteriorating trend into to the deepest error
in Church history. Christian anti-Semitism has been
strengthened by the mistaken view that the Bible did not
mean what it said. Origen's teaching suggested that deeper

---

[43] The *Hexapla* was a parallel version of the Hebrew text of
the Old Testament, the *Septuagint*, a transliteration in Greek, and
three Greek translations of the Old Testament. The Greek versions
came from Symmachus, Theodotion, and Aquila (see footnote 10 and
comments about Onkelos and Aquila). Origen used the *Hexapla* for
his interpretations of the Old Testament. *Eerdman's Handbook to
the History of Christianity*, p. 104.

[44] Eusebius, Pamphilus, *The Ecclesiastical History of*,
Translated by Christian Frederick Cruse, (Grand Rapids, Michigan,
Baker Book House, 1992), p. 226.

spiritual truth was contained in the words of the text which needed to be discovered by the interpreter. If Church fathers had not ignored or allegorized God's written covenant to Israel, the despicable actions of later Christian anti-Semites may have been tempered by truth. The objective truth of the Bible clearly shows God's love for the Jews. Unfortunately, scholars like Origen, who were prone to an allegorical twist, determined that the Bible meant what the Church leaders said it meant. The allegorical method avoided investigation into original intent and context. The interpreter sought to make his own subjective view the primary tool of biblical interpretation. Subjective analysis never leads to objectivity.

CHAPTER VIII

ROME'S MISTAKE & ISRAEL'S PAIN

The inspired authors of Scripture communicated exactly what God desired for the nurturing and growth of His Church. Too often, then as now, Christian leaders have presumed to speak for God while infusing their own perspectives into His text. The loss of objectivity can be destructive to those who depend on their leaders for direction. Faithful followers deserve objective truth from God's Word. Religious rhetoric is not sufficient to guide believers in matters of faith and practice. God expects accuracy from His servants who handle His Word and minister His truth. His message was carefully preserved in His written Word for His chosen (Jewish and non-Jewish) people. Scripture serves to inform, reform, and transform humanity, never to conform to humanity or the changing views of the Church.

Until the time of Origen, literal readings of the Bible were commonplace. Origen changed to a standard of interpretation foreign to most Jewish and Christian predecessors. The literal method of Bible interpretation goes back to Ezra and the time of the return from the Babylonian exile. The nation of Israel had forgotten much of their language and their Scriptures. A literal method of interpreting God's Word to His people seemed to be the best choice. Ezra's literal methods were continued by Jews until the time of Jesus.[45] An example of this can be seen in rabbinic thought which expected a literal Messiah to come and free the first century Jews from Roman oppression.

Important questions arose concerning the interpretation of the Old Testament prophecies surrounding Israel. Should they be taken literally, or were they to be spiritualized and applied to the Church? Stated differently, did the Church replace Israel as heir to the promises, and, therefore, do the Bible prophecies and promises contained in the Old Testament transfer exclusively to the Church? The answer to this question influences one's analysis of Scripture and impacts how Bible prophecy is understood. It is the purpose of a good system of hermeneutics to determine the original meaning of the Bible. Obviously,

----

[45] It appears that Philo of Alexandria, the ancient Jewish philosopher, paved the way for allegorical interpretations in the Church. Hellenistic Judaism incorporated many elements of Hellenistic culture. Dan Cohn-Sherbok writes, "Paradoxically, this quest in the Greco-Roman period provided the basis for Christianity's eventual spiritualization of Scripture and its consequent antithetical attitude to rabbinic Judaism." *The Crucified Jew*, p. 4.

with such divergent opinions surrounding eschatology, some must be right while others are wrong. Studying to know truth requires a proper approach and discipline. Two basic yet significantly different approaches exist. One has already been briefly discussed as the allegorical method. The other approach is known as the grammatical-historical method, hereinafter referred to as literal.

Under Origen's allegorical method, moral and spiritual meanings were added to the original intent. The spiritualized interpretation of Scripture took precedence over the original message which the inspired authors intended to communicate. Some leaders within the Church defined textual intent in parallel with the then current doctrines of the Church. Those leaders conveniently read and interpreted biblical texts in light of accepted Church doctrine and authority. As errors developed within the faith and practices of the Church, those errors found justification within the allegorical interpretations of the spiritual leaders. Instead of the Church being changed by the life-changing Word of God, the Church changed the meaning of God's Word. Churchmen with a vested interest in the retention of authority, held sway to the reading and interpreting of the Bible within the Church. Their methods of interpreting texts led to support for their preferred doctrinal positions. Power and presumption ruled where proper hermeneutics should have served. Theories of interpretation which were supportive of popular doctrines gained the largest acceptance. The Bible was forced into a supportive role to uphold the regnant belief system. Hal Lindsey addressed the results of Origen's allegorical interpretations to expose the error.

> Using this method of prophetic interpretation, Church theologians began to develop the idea that the Israelites had permanently forfeited all their covenants by rejecting Jesus as the Messiah. This view taught that these covenants now belong to the Church, and that it is the only true Israel now and forever. The view also taught that the Jews will never again have a future as a Divinely chosen people, and that the Messiah will never establish His Messianic Kingdom on earth that was promised to them.[46]

Changing the Guard

The Gentile converts to Jewish Christianity in the early centuries took over and replaced Jewish leadership. This was a natural phenomenon as the ratio of Gentiles grew in proportion to Jewish Church membership. As the decades turned to centuries, the Church disabled, dismembered, and finally discarded its previous Jewish influences. Grievously, as the Jews disappeared from Church leadership, some truths of Scripture were lost to the Church. Gentile leaders faced organizational, political,

---

[46] Lindsey, p. 8.

financial, and spiritual dilemmas. They were forced to evaluate issues that were new to their changing character and demography. Post-apostolic Christianity moved away from Jerusalem-centered influence and drew closer to the influence of Rome.

Naturally, Gentile churchmen looked for methods to encourage themselves during the difficult years of the transformation. Many questions surfaced as a result of that transformation from a Jewish to a predominantly Gentile group. Christian history shows evidence that their answers were incorrect.

"What was Israel?" "Who inherited the promises of God to Israel?" "Was there a difference between natural and spiritual Israel?" "Did God's attitude change in relation to His covenant with Israel?" Even questions about God's attitude toward mankind came into focus. "Did a metamorphosis transpire from the Old Testament God of the Law to the New Testament God of Grace?" "If so, what became of God's viscious judgments and visitations on sin?" The previously perceived chosenness of the Jews had become an embarrassing distraction to some within the Church. By their very existence, the Jewish people inadvertently became an undermining force.

The efforts to assert a new Gentile chosenness by Gentile Church leaders led to the devaluation of Jewish chosenness. Eventually, the view toward divine Jewish chosenness was replaced with a view toward cursed Jewish exclusion. In fact, the Jewish race was in the way.

He That Endures

The Church could not be the sole heir of the Father and of His kingdom promises so long as the primogeniture existed in a legitimate Jewish first born race of Children of God. Perhaps that is the reason that the Church has been trying to reduce the Jewish people to orphan status for 1,800 years. Leaders in the Church determined to steal the hope, the position, and the inheritance promised to the Jews. While moving into their covenant relationship with God, the Gentiles intentionally excluded the Jews. Doctrinal error, not God's written Word, led to manifestations of hatred. Jesus wept over Jerusalem when He thought of the pain His people would experience. Now He might weep over His follower's lack of love toward His people.

From these attitudes evolved the idea that they were blind impostors under the curse of God, and unrepentant Christ-killers. Their tenacious efforts to remain a separate and distinct race with the hope of the Messiah's future coming to establish a promised Kingdom of God were viewed as a special arrogance. The Church leaders saw no justification for the Jews to remain a distinct people, since in their view, their hopes belonged exclusively to the Church forever.[47]

Their error led to a steady deterioration of truth.

> The Church began to see itself as God's true Israel, the inheritor of the covenant promises made to Israel, then in the eyes of the Church, the Israelites ceased to have any legitimate purpose or right to exist as a people. Again, it is important to note that the only way the Church could arrive at this view was by interpreting prophecy allegorically. From this error in eschatology (the doctrine of last things or prophecy) to outright anti-Semitism was only a matter of time.[48]

It can be deduced from the teachings of Origen and Saint Augustine that Church leaders came to a view that the Jews were a lost race without hope of redemption. This "new" theology was contrary to the teachings which immediately followed Jesus, the disciples, and the charter members of the Church. Christian anti-Semitism would have been both absurd and abhorrent to Jesus Christ. As previously discussed, when the Church determined that Israel had forfeited their covenants by rejecting Christ, their view provided for a dramatic shift in their eschatology.

---

[47] Lindsey, p. 8.

[48] Ibid., p. 9.

They taught that all the future messianic promises of Israel were then transferred to the new Israel, the Church.

The Roman Catholic Church, using Origen's system of interpretation and Augustine's theology, soon applied and instituted the teaching that they were the inheritors of Israel's promises-- that they were the inheritors of the Kingdom promised to Israel and therefore must take ultimate authority over the political powers of this world. At one point during the Middle Ages, the Church held authority over virtually all the rulers of Europe. History witnesses that this was one of the most oppressive periods of Christianity, both toward the Christians and those outside of the Church. These prophetic views were a complete departure from the original teachings of the Apostolic Fathers of the Church, whose period extended from A.D. 33 to shortly after A.D. 100.[49]

The qualifications for an Apostolic Father were to include having been either among the original apostles and disciples or were discipled directly by men of this group who themselves were first-hand witnesses to the glory and truth of Christ. In other words, the Apostolic Fathers were taught by Jesus or the disciples of Jesus. Therefore, as "students," the Apostolic Fathers had highly qualified "professors."

---

[49] Ibid., pp. 9-10.

Certainly, men like Origen were brilliant, dedicated, and creative. Nonetheless, Origen and his protégés followed others. Their predecessors were the Apostolic Fathers. They were chronologically, theologically, geographically, and experientially closer to Jesus than Origen. The erroneous anti-Semitic notions that developed after the Church accepted allegorical views of Scripture reveal that much more than time separated those later doctors of the Church from Christ. The Apostolic Fathers would have rejected Origen's and Augustine's allegorical interpretations and their attitudes toward the Jewish people.

Jesus would certainly have declared that He did not reject the Jewish people. The sin of a Jew is no more taxing to the blood of Jesus than the sin of a Gentile. The sins of any people group require the same cure, the atoning blood of Christ. Jesus would have had a prompt response if queried about His view of anti-Semitism, even during His last moments alive among the Jewish people. He would have called anti-Semitism a sin because He bled for repentant Jews and Jew-haters alike. Error entered the Church in the form of Christian anti-Semitism because Christ's attitude toward the Jewish people was either overlooked or misunderstood.

Sadly, this seed of error continued under the guidance of Aurelius Augustinus, the bishop of Hippo (354 - 430), better known as Saint Augustine. The leaders of the Church during the fourth century slid further into error in relation to Jewish considerations. It then became even worse.

By the early fifth century, the Church believed that it was the sole possessor of Israel's covenant promises, including the ownership of the promised land. Acting from this false premise, the Church began to use its new political power to create and enforce anti-Jewish legislation--a practice that became usual in the Middle Ages. In many cases throughout the Middle Ages, the institutional Church either forced Jews to convert by political oppression and terror, or put them to the sword.[50]

Augustine established a method of interpretation that insisted the Bible be read in a manner always consistent with established Church doctrine. If a biblical idea did not fit into Church policy, the interpretation was wrong. "Mystical" interpretations were incorporated to fit the purposes of the Church.

The God of the Old Testament, in a sense, became an embarrassment to the Church. They just did not like all the "bad" things that God did. Their view of God made it harder and harder for them to believe that He destroyed armies, crushed cities, violently punished offenders, sent plagues, rained fire and brimstone, and sent a flood to wipe

---

[50] Ibid., pp. 12-13.

out most of the human race. The Christian God of love sent peace not fire. Psalms of praise were understandable. In contrast, imprecatory Psalms[51] created questions about the character of the author. The Old Testament was too Jewish in its orientation to satisfy the needs of the fourth century Gentile Church which desired to assert its own preeminence as the rightful repository of truth. Some Church leaders wanted to discard the entire Old Testament. Others, like Augustine, chose to force their ideas into the meaning of the Old Testament text to avoid being confronted with the reality of the text.

<u>Overemphasis in Christology</u>

Finding Christ in the Old Testament became urgent. Some manipulated the Old Testament until it was used as an enormous pronouncement of the Messiah. This exaggerated emphasis further reduced the importance of

---

[51] Just as the Book of Psalms contains songs of praise to God, along with glorious enthronement Psalms, and wonderful Psalms of Messianic hope, the imprecatory Psalms called for punishment and curses to fall upon the enemies of Israel. There are many imprecatory Psalms that create an image of violent judgment that look to a God of vengeance. This image of God is frustrating to readers who only concern themselves with an incomplete view of God. It is true that God reaches out to His children in love. It is also true that the same hands that hold a child in love, punish a child for correction. Examples of imprecatory Psalms include: Psalms 58, 83, 109, and 137. The last example graphically offers a prayer for God to permit the Babylonians to be destroyed and bring joy at smashing the Babylonian babies "against the rock" (Psalm 137:9).

the people of the book. Whereas Jesus was certainly proclaimed and foretold by the prophets, the Old Testament offered more than a messianic witness. Speaking of God's view of Abraham and the Jewish forefathers, Augustine suggests that

> God so accounted of these men, and at that time made them such heralds of His Son, that not only in what they said, but in what they did, or what happened to them, Christ is sought, Christ is found. Whatever Scripture saith of Abraham, both happened and is a prophecy.[52]

Augustine transformed the purpose of actual events in the life of Abraham to little more than messianic declarations. Instead of seeing God's historical actions toward the Jewish patriarchs, hidden messages about Jesus were sought. Unfortunately, modern interpreters are often guilty of the same erroneous emphasis. Contrary to the teaching of some, Christ is not to be seen in every Old Testament event. Some biblical events were simply historical events. No messianic mysteries, types, or shadows were intended in the golden hemorrhoids of the Philistines at Ashdod recorded in first Samuel 6:4. The overemphasis of Christology in Old Testament studies is little more than another method of ignoring the people of

---

[52] Augustine, *The Confessions of St. Augustine*, Translated by E. B. Pusey, in footnote number 2, (J. M. Dent & Sons Ltd., New York, 1920), pp. 42-43.

the book. The Jewish people are still the people of the book, and they are still relevant. God's Jewish messengers have carried a Jewish message to His Jewish people. Students of the Bible should realize that the book has inherent value beyond the message of a first century Messiah and a final century Armageddon. There are the people in the middle!

> Less than 2 percent of Old Testament prophecy is messianic. Less than 5 percent specifically describes the New Covenant age. Less than 1 percent concerns events yet to come.[53]

This should correct interpreters who teach that Jesus has been portrayed in most events of the Old Testament. They need to review their methods of interpretation. According to the calculations of Gordon Fee and Douglas Stuart, ninety-eight percent of the Old Testament texts are not messianic. Interpreters must also grapple with the fact that ninety-five percent of the Old Testament texts do not describe the New Testament era. Additionally, it is needful to reevaluate many eschatological views in light of the fact

----

[53] Gordon Fee and Douglas Stuart, *How to Read the Bible for All its Worth*, (Zondervan Publishing House, Grand Rapids, Michigan, 1993), p. 166.

that ninety-nine percent of prophecy has already been fulfilled.[54]

The Gentile Church grew up in the pagan Greco-Roman world. They saw that the Old Testament books were written by Jews, about Jews, and for Jews. To some, it may have appeared as though the non-Jews were considered as an afterthought. It became too troublesome. Something had to be done. Men like Origen and Augustine took the more appealing route and simply interpreted the text to fit their popular view of God. This concept of loosely handling the Word of God did not completely envelop the Christian world. The school of Antioch did have some thinkers who promoted accurate biblical exegesis. These men, however, were classed as heretics. Although Augustine made significant contributions[55] that

---

[54] These numbers (used for emphasis) are the inverse of the statistics presented by Gordon Fee and Douglas Stuart.

[55] Saint Augustine did provide the Church with many positive perspectives, and he gave the world of literature one of its greatest works. The story of his conversion to Christianity is the first authentic autobiography accepted in literary circles from the ancient world. His reflections and perceptions open up worlds of thought to the readers of his *Confessions* (written in 397 CE). As one of the doctors of the Church, he gave additional contributions that must also be considered. "In his doctrines of sin and grace, he went far beyond the earlier theologians, taught an unconditional election of grace, and restricted the purposes of redemption to the definite circle of the elect. It will not be denied by anyone acquainted with Church History that Augustine was an eminently great and good man, and that his labors and writings contributed more to the promotion of sound doctrine and

benefitted the Church, he also successfully promoted what Origen had perverted and Justin Martyr had invented. Christian anti-Semitism thrived alongside the practice of allegorical methods of Scripture interpretation. This tragic approach to interpreting the Bible lasted over 1,000 years. It became the dominant method until the time of the Reformation.

Throughout the Middle Ages, anti-Semitism came to the world from the Church. Augustine contributed to an anti-Semitic attitude in the Church.

Augustine had taught two important things which were to become widely quoted and applied during the Middle Ages. First, he taught that the Jews should be allowed to live among the Christian communities because their wretched circumstances were an evidence of the truthfulness of the Old Testament prophecies that predicted their rejection and dispersion. Second he taught, on the basis of his allegorical interpretation of Psalm 59:12, that the Jews should nevertheless be restricted in their privileges and continually humiliated.[56]

---

the revival of true religion than did those of any other man between Paul and Luther. Prior to Augustine's day the time had been largely taken up in correcting heresies within the Church and in refuting attacks from the pagan world in which it found itself." Loraine Boettner, *The Reformed Doctrine of Predestination*, (Presbyterian and Reformed Publishing Company, Phillipsburg, New Jersey, 1932), pp. 365-366.

[56] Lindsey, p. 13.

DOES JACOB'S TROUBLE WEAR A CROSS?

God's words from the Hebrew Bible to the Children of Israel had gone unheeded by Roman Christianity. God's love for the Jews was conveniently ignored by men, though acknowledged by God. Within their ancient history, when the Jews chose a human king over the kingship of God their arrogance did not impact their ultimate standing with God. As related by Samuel, "For the LORD will not forsake His people for His great name's sake, because it hath pleased the LORD to make you a people unto Himself" (1 Samuel 12:22). Had Onkelos lived long enough, he would have seen the stock value of Judaism decrease even further in the eyes of many Christians. Jews were devaluated to the unpleasant position of spiritually bankrupt and worthy of death. The Christian world degenerated into a monstrous example of intolerance and violence. From Constantine to Augustine, through the Crusades, and into the Reformation, Jews were consistently depreciated, attacked, and even destroyed in the name of Christ.

During the Reformation, Martin Luther fought for a change from some specific Catholic practices. The anti-Semitic writings quoted earlier from Luther's works could leave one with an incomplete view of that great Reformer. This would not be just. In spite of his erroneous views of Jews and Judaism, his contributions to the cause of Christianity should not be devalued.

Relating to some of the primary methods of Scripture interpretation, it should be remembered that it was Martin Luther who put forth the teaching that Scripture interprets itself. Luther realized that churchmen had wantonly misinterpreted the Bible. That significant change in understanding brought revolutionary adjustments to the Church. Ultimately, the Bible was restored to the common people. Later, the response of the Catholic Church brought their own Counter Reformation. In total, these events led to tremendous improvements and benefits experienced by millions of people around the world. Unfortunately, Jews were rarely the beneficiaries of Christian advancement.

CHAPTER IX

CHRISTIANITY, A JEWISH RELIGION

Unfortunately, the Jewishness of the early Church has been nearly forgotten. If the Gentile Church had a better recollection of its own beginnings, the darkness of Christian anti-Semitism would be forced into the light and broadly questioned. The historicity of the original Jewish nature of Christianity is genuine and well documented. The corpus of compelling evidence to support this idea includes the various Gospel accounts and New Testament depictions of life in the early Church of Jewish believers. It is from this Jewish culture that the Gentile Church has grown. These historically valuable writings often revolve around Jewish festivals, customs, and Temple or synagogal[57] worship. The Jewish nature of Christianity is

---

[57] In contradistinction, there was only one Temple which was in Jerusalem, whereas there were many synagogues. The holy site for all of the sacrificial and ceremonial rites for observant Jews took place exclusively at the Jerusalem Temple. Synagogues were a later development which grew out of the necessity for a place to worship during the Babylonian exile of the Jewish people from Judah and

unquestionable, and the Jewish nature of the earliest Christian writings is profound.

The only source of Scripture that was read by the early Church came from teachings within their Jewish heritage. Truth was sought in the sacred writings of Judaism. The Torah that was studied in synagogues was also revered as the sacred writings studied by men of the early Church. Even texts from the Jewish Apocrypha and Pseudepigrapha were read and valued by early Church Fathers, and even earlier by the writers of the New Testament. This is known because there are references from Jewish non-canonical works such as "The Assumption of Moses" and "I Enoch" in the New Testament. Some scholars believe that both works were quoted in the Epistle of Jude. "Jude explicitly quotes Enoch and introduces the quotation with the formula 'Enoch, the seventh from Adam, prophesied, saying' " (found in Jude 14-15).[58] Jude also refers to the non-canonical text of The Assumption of Moses. The

---

Israel. Those Jews who chose to live in the Diaspora after the exile ended maintained the use of synagogues within their later practices. The Temple remained as the only approved site for much of the religious requirements of the Jewish people. Outside of Jerusalem, the people worshipped and gathered in synagoues.

[58] H. F. D. Sparks, Editor, *The Apocryphal Old Testament.* (Oxford University Press, Oxford, 1990), p.169.

discussion arose about the body of Moses and the archangel Michael disputed with the devil but "dared not bring against him a reviling accusation, but said, 'the Lord rebuke you!'" (Jude 9). "More details about this dispute may be gleaned from other Fathers, some of whom explicitly name the Assumption as their source."[59]

Early Church Fathers were not in complete agreement as to what should be included in the canon. Many of the writings which were important to the Jews (both Jewish Christians as well as the rabbinic Jews) were important to the original Gentile Christians. Some were so important that they were viewed as potential candidates for inclusion into the New Testament. Sources as important to the early Church as Tertullian and Origen accepted Enoch. St. Augustine "admitted that Enoch had written 'not a little' by divine inspiration."[60]

Though most Protestants disregard the Apocrypha, it had meaning to Jesus. He visited the Temple to celebrate the Feast of Dedication (John 10:22). This commemoration of the reconsecration of the Temple, after the desecration by the Syrians, was taught to the Jewish people from the apocryphal <u>Book of the Maccabees</u>.

---

[59] Ibid., p. 602.

[60] Ibid., p. 170. Quotation taken from Augustine's *Civ. Dei,* xv. 23, xviii. 38.

Apostles Without Bibles

These facts serve to illustrate the vast difference between the sources of study materials of the Jewish founders from those of modern Gentile Christians. <u>The New Testament Church did not even have a New Testament</u>.

The Apostles could not easily carry the holy scrolls around on their missionary journeys so they read the Jewish Bible in the Jewish synagogues. Modern Gentile Christians might wonder, "How did the Apostles accomplish so much with so little?"

These Apostles cast new light on ancient texts and as a result they had the faith, hope, love, and enthusiasm to evangelize much of the known world. Truth had a profound affect on those in the early Church. Revolutionary understandings were developed. Exciting relationships were brought forth between the prophecies of the Hebrew Bible and the teaching which the apostles brought to the emerging New Testament Church. In turn, the New Testament Church had a profound affect on its world. Bold soldiers of the cross engaged in new forms of spiritual warfare as new understandings were gleaned from ancient writings. They had a secret weapon in their arsenal to aid them in their interpretation of the Bible. They knew

Jesus and they had His Holy Spirit. Still, problems surfaced within a few generations after the Apostles.

Jews for Jesus in the First Century

The Jewishness of Christian experience was intact during the Sub-Apostolic Era. This period is identified as extending from approximately 100 CE until approximately 156 CE. This time specifically "extends from the death of the Apostle John (around 100 A.D.) to the death of his disciple, Polycarp (155-156 A.D.)."[61] *The Teaching of the Twelve Apostles*, better known as the *Didache*, was an important document which helped early believers during the generation after the Apostles. It was not actually written by the Apostles themselves.[62] Rather, it is believed that these were the teachings of the Apostles. The *Didache* is considered by many to be authentic and accurate. Eusebius and Clement of Alexandria knew of the document, therefore its age and authenticity is accepted. Teachings contained within the *Didache* do not express significant contradictions to the Jewish form of original Apostolic Christianity.

---

[61] Seif, pp. 215-216.

[62] The dating of the *Didache* is uncertain. Some scholars believe that it was written as early as 50 CE, although it is more likely to have been composed toward the end of the first century. Later dates have been suggested, nonetheless, it is certainly one of the oldest authentic works of the Early Church.

DOES JACOB'S TROUBLE WEAR A CROSS?

Incredible significance can be identified in the historical record provided by Eusebius on the early leadership of the Church. He preserves the list which details the succession of leaders in the Church. Eusebius reports the important fact that "The first fifteen bishops were all Hebrews."[63] The claim of the Catholic Church suggests that an unbroken line of Popes can be followed back to Peter. Considering the identification and lineage of the original fifteen Hebrew bishops, some modern Catholics might have an interesting response to this fact.

> There were fifteen successions of bishops in that church, all which, they say, were Hebrews from the first, and received the knowledge of Christ pure and unadulterated; so that, in the estimation of those who were able to judge they were well approved, and worthy of the episcopal office. For at that time the whole church under them, consisted of faithful Hebrews who continued from the time of the apostles.[64]

Unfortunately, after the Hebrews lost control of the position of bishop, they never regained the position or influence.

Before Paul was the Apostle to the Gentiles, he was Saul of Tarsus, a Jew. Most of the disciples were Jewish. Most of the Bible, Old Testament and New Testament, was

---

[63] Eusebius, p. 475.

[64] Ibid., p. 130.

written by Jews and most of the early Church members were Jewish. Jesus, His siblings, and His parents were also Jewish. Equally relevant, He was well versed in synagogal worship. Jesus ministered to Jewish people in a Jewish land. He was involved in Jewish customs, spoke in the Jewish language, and related in terms of Jewish concepts. He made pilgrimages to the Jewish center of worship during certain Jewish pilgrimage festivals.[65] The Jewishness of Jesus should not surprise modern readers. What might surprise them is that if Jewish Paul had not successfully contextualized the Jewish story of a Jewish Messiah in his effort to carry it into the pagan Greco-Roman world of his era, the Church may have continued to grow within the Jewish fold with much less friction.

The Jewish Christians of the early days desired to coexist with other Jews. They were not immediately kicked out of the Temple or the synagogues beyond Jerusalem as some may believe. James, the Jewish head of the first Church in Jerusalem, was known to be a solid man of prayer and Temple worship. "James the Lord's brother, for example, was admired by many non-Christian Jews for his constant fasting and prayer."[66] The Jerusalem Council

---

[65] A few examples of these are: Chanukah (Feast of the Dedication, John 10:22); Succoth (Feast of Tabernacles, John 7:2, which included the water libation ceremony referred to in John 7:37); and Pesach (Passover), when Jesus celebrated the Last Supper.

[66] Dowley, p. 204.

was concerned that the incoming Gentile converts would jeapordize the Jewish Christians' relationships with non-believing Jews. F. F. Bruce suggests that the influx of Gentiles caused problems for the Jewish Christians and "provides a sufficient explanation of their sudden unpopularity with many Jews who had formerly respected them."[67]

Christianity, a Jewish Phenomenon

Paul often attended synagogue services where he worshipped with the Jewish people. Many synagogues even let him preach for a while. Contrary to common accusations against Paul, he did not discredit Judaism, Jewish people, or Jewish worship. He reverenced the Jewish Torah and remained a Jew. He regularly attended synagogue on his travels. A few examples of this are: in Salamis, Acts 13: 5; in Antioch, Acts 13:14; in Iconium, Acts 14:1; in Thessalonica, Acts 17:1; in Berea, Acts 17:10; in Athens, Acts 17:17; in Corinth, Acts 18:4; and in Ephesus, Acts 18:19. The synagogues were familiar and convenient to Paul. It was not abnormal for Paul to use them as a base of operations upon entering a new mission area.

---

[67] F. F. Bruce, *New Testament History*, (A Doubleday-Galilee Book, Garden City, New York, 1980), p. 261.

To those outside of Judaism, Christianity was another group of Jews. Some would suggest that view from the outside continued for centuries.

> Until the year 325 c.e. the Christians were considered to be a Jewish sect, and they had a large following in the country. Debates between the orthodox and Christian Jews were a common occurrence.[68]

Then, as now, a variety of opinions were common within Judaism. Disagreement was acceptable and commonplace. Although Jesus did not agree with all facets of Judaism or the Jewish leaders, He was a Jew. In his book *The Origin of the Christian Faith*, Jeffrey Seif says, "Though He indeed was bodily resurrected some two thousand years ago, it may be said that His Jewish heritage was executed, buried, and has yet to fully arise."[69]

The record of discord is recognized in the New Testament by the Judaizer's concerns over what level of Judaic requirements were needed to be included in the lives of new adherents to their Jewish sect. The account in the Acts of the Apostles shows how truly Jewish they were. Their concerns were intended to insure acceptance among their Jewish associates. They were not trying to protect their families. They were not trying to protect their jobs.

---

[68] Bader, p. 462.

[69] Seif, p. 15.

They were not trying to insure their safety. The Jerusalem Council was concerned about losing their credibility among the practicing Jews of Jerusalem. All of the above concerns were issues faced by Jewish Christians, but always foremost they were committed to maintaining a proper stance among their people. The truth of the Gospel was never compromised, but the Torah was upheld. The Torah was always the basis for faith in Christ. They were conscious of the fact that their words, actions, attitudes, teachings, and doctrines were under constant scrutiny by the Jewish leaders, as well as the Jewish people who watched the emerging Church developing in their midst. They did not want Jewish Christianity to be devalued in the eyes of their fellowmen due to the Gentiles lack of understanding or commitment to Torah.

In apostolic times, most non-Jews were pagans, as paganism was the established religion of the Roman Empire. The Jews were aware of the fact that in prior generations pagan idolatry had brought judgment from God. The Church leaders realized that they could not permit pagan influences of the era to enter their sect. That would have amplified the Jewish accusations that they had left the faith to worship other gods. The hint of perceived disregard for the law would have served their detractors. They realized this potential depreciation would further separate them from their Jewish countrymen who did not get involved with pagans. They did not want anything to impede their ability to reach the lost sheep of the house of Israel that Jesus came to seek and save. The Jerusalem Jewish Christians were concerned about their Jewish mission field. With this view under consideration, a reevaluation of the words spoken to Paul by his Jewish Christian brothers in the Council help to show their pervasive involvement in Jewish life. "You see brother, how many myriads of Jews there are who have believed, and they are zealous for the law" (Acts 21: 20). From their Jerusalem headquarters, these zealous Jewish Christians had access to many unbelieving Jews. The leaders at headquarters did not want any newly recruited Gentile Christians to hinder their ministry opportunities through an ill-conceived *faux pax*.

The significant question facing Jewish believers within nascent Christianity was not of Judaism being purged from the Church; rather, the Church leaders (with no less an authority than the very brother of Jesus initially presiding) were correctly seeking assurances that the world would not creep in and pollute the purity of Jesus' original Jewish Christianity.

Jesus lived out a Jewish form of worship and practice. That form of Christianity which Christ shared with the Disciples was the Jewish form of the faith that won the early Jewish converts. William Whiston makes a bold, revealing comment about the impact of early Jewish Christianity among the Jewish people. In Whiston's

DOES JACOB'S TROUBLE WEAR A CROSS?

dissertation on *The Testimonies Of Josephus Concerning Jesus Christ, John The Baptist And James The Just, Vindicated*, he indicates that faith in Jesus was a growing phenomenon among ancient Jewish people. Whiston suggests, "that there were many ten thousands of Jews, who were persuaded that he was the Christ of God, who was foretold by the prophets."[70] Whiston refers to Acts 21:20 in support of his view. Josephus, the Jewish historian, identified that Jesus was a "teacher of such men as receive the truth with pleasure. He drew over to him both many of the Jews, and many of the Gentiles."[71]

---

[70] Josephus, Flavius, translated by William Whiston, *The Works of Josephus: New Updated Edition.* (Hendrickson Publishers, Inc., Massachusetts, 1993), pp. 815-815.

[71] Ibid., p. 480.

CHAPTER X

ANTI-JUDAISM

It would be a mistake to suggest that Judaism was abhorred by their pre-Christian contemporaries. Unfortunately, anti-Semitism was a uniquely "Christian" development that did not exist until the Church formulated the view that the Jews were guilty of deicide. That errant belief was unknown prior to the dark ages of early Gentile Christianity. Among some segments of the ancient non-Christian population, Judaism was highly respected. This truth is imperative to understanding a correct view of the relationship between ancient Judaism, ancient paganism, and ancient Christianity. Between the second century BCE and the end of the first century CE, although anti-Judaism existed, some Gentiles had a view toward philo-Judaism.

> The period . . . witnessed the development of
> admiration and veneration for many Jewish rituals
> and ideas. It was the age of philo-Judaism as well
> as anti-Judaism, of conversion to Judaism as well
> as hatred of Judaism. Although the Jews sought
> to keep themselves separate and distinct, they
> were also eager to accept and retain gentile
> converts. Indeed, some of the anti-Jewish

literature of this period is motivated
. . . by a desire to discourage conversion to
Judaism. The literature that evinces a dislike of
Judaism paradoxically confirms Judaism's
powerful attraction.[72]

Anti-Judaism existed among the Gentiles, however it
was a much different form than is generally understood.

Furthermore, the social and economic
tensions that produced the virulent anti-Semitism
of nineteenth- and twentieth-century Europe did
not exist in antiquity. There were no "nation-
states" in antiquity in which the Jews were an
unassimilable foreign element. The Jews of
antiquity had a variegated economic life in both
the diaspora and the land of Israel. They were
farmers, laborers, artisans, soldiers, etc. Most of
them, like the vast majority of the people of
antiquity, were very poor. Not a single ancient
text says or implies that the Jews are hated or
feared because of their economic power. Money-
lending was still centuries in the future, and the
rise of the Jewish middle classes did not begin
until the nineteenth century.[73]

---

[72] Ibid., p. 49.

[73] Shaye J. D. Cohen, *From the Maccabees to the Mishnah*,
(The Waestminster Press, Philadelphia, 1987), p. 48.

<u>The God-Fearers</u>

The original form of Christianity, which was Jewish Christianity, worked extremely well for Jews and Gentiles as shown by the success of that form of Christianity during the New Testament era. Many of the early Gentile converts came from the ranks of those Gentiles known as "God-fearers," and there were many in synagogue worship. It was the Jewishness of Christianity that drew many Gentiles to the faith.

Prior to Christianity, Judaism had been well oriented toward mission activities.

In the Greco-Roman period Judaism became missionary in outlook and attempted to establish itself as a universal religion. Proselytes were to be considered as enjoying the same status as born-Jews, and numerous "God-fearers" (sympathizers to Judaism) were attracted to the synagogue.[74]

The "God-fearers" had been loosely joined to Judaism without becoming proselytes to the faith. The Church offered the best elements of Judaism without the difficult entry requirements. The good news of Christianity contained the teachings of Judaism without circumcision. Judaism, with its basis of virtuous laws and ethical teachings, presented a more desirable lifestyle than the Pagan religion of Rome. Gentiles who were already

---

[74] Cohn-Sherbok, p. 3.

predisposed to an appreciation for the monotheistic and moral elements of Judaism saw a wonderful alternative in Christianity. It was the perfect opportunity to enter the "better" life of Judaism, the eternal promises of Christianity, and escape the debauchery of paganism.

God's Open Door

God's plan of salvation provided for a broader audience than the Children of Israel. This was one of the focal points of the good news of the Gospel. The New Testament, and the historical facts of what has occured since the Resurrection, prove that God's intention was to bring the non-Jewish world into His loving arms. Truly, the Jews of the era did not enmasse accept Jesus. Still, if many Jews had not received Jesus, the Church would not have been born. With trepidation and the clear move of the Holy Spirit, the Jewish Church conditionally welcomed Gentiles into their fellowship. The door was opened to the Gentiles. The Gentile world was given the opportunity to become part of the family of God. The time was approaching for the words of the ancient Hebrew prophet Isaiah to be fulfilled,

> For the earth shall be full of the knowledge of the Lord, As the waters cover the sea. And in that day there shall be a Root of Jesse, Who shall stand as a banner to the people; For the Gentiles shall seek Him, And His resting place shall be glorious (Isaiah 11: 9b-10 NKJV).

God created a new opportunity for the Gentiles when He sent Peter to Cornelius (Acts 10). Peter's unwillingness to associate with non-Jews was changed by a supernatural vision described in Acts. Perhaps the most revolutionary event since Calvary took place at the home of Cornelius as Peter obeyed the commands of God which followed that vision. In a sense, God had been the God of the Jews, and after that experience with Cornelius, non-Jews heard and accepted the Gospel. Peter had a revelation and he understood the fact that God was not "a respecter of persons" (Acts 10:34 KJV). The Jewish leadership of the Church saw that fact as a revolution. The concept was previously foreign to normative Judaism. It was also questioned within normative Christianity shortly after Jesus. God opened up the Jewish phenomenon of Christianity to the Gentile world through the same sign He had shown to the original Jewish believers at Pentecost. The Holy Spirit came upon the Gentiles.

Prior to Peter's sensational proclamation, the Gentiles were rarely engaged in Jewish Christian endeavors. The Judaean apostles were obviously surprised and shocked by Peter's behavior. Sharing the Gospel with non-Jews was not a practice of the Church. They would not even eat together, let alone worship and experience Christ together. Peter reported to the Jewish Church leaders that he had gone to the Gentiles because "The Spirit told me to have no hesitation about going with them"

DOES JACOB'S TROUBLE WEAR A CROSS?

(Acts 11:12 NIV). Peter went, but it is likely that he had hesitations. God showed him the original vision three times to insure Peter's receptivity to the message. It was a drastic change for Peter, the Jews, and the Gentiles.

God had opened the way of salvation to the Gentiles by showing His willingness to permit the merging of the Jewish world with the non-Jewish world into a new broader union forming the Christian Church. Jesus was Lord over the Jews and Lord over the Gentiles. He was Lord over Jerusalem and Lord over Rome. The Father's resurrected Son was made Lord over the earth and Lord over heaven. It was as though the Kingdom of God was breaking into the kingdom of this world. This broader union within the Church had previously not been defined in terms understood by God's people. God chose to impact a new audience with His special relationship. God invited the Gentiles into His family on an equal basis with the Jews.

Prior to Jesus, Gentiles were considered alien to His promises. Whether the Gentile entry into the family of God is seen as a revelation or a revolution, at a minimum, it provided the opportunity for the Gentiles to become the majority voice of the Church. God led the Gentiles into the Church. Within a short time they took over the Church and removed Jewish leadership and influence from their form of worship and practice. As has been previously shown, by the second century the Jews were out of power; by the fourth century they were out of favor.

Increasingly Christians came to regard Jews as deliberate haters of good. When the church became recognized by Constantine, legal discrimination against Jews increased and they were gradually deprived of all rights.[75]

---

[75] Dowley, p. 50.

CHAPTER XI

THE CALL OF JEALOUSY

One of the greatest facts of the New Testament is seen in the change with which God chose to relate to a predominantly Gentile world. This change may be viewed as signifying a type of new dispensation in God's plan whereby the Gentiles were offered entry into relationship with God. Though the Gentiles had been widely accepted into Jewish Christianity, no reason existed to suggest that they would replace the original people of God's choice. No need existed for Gentile Christians to displace the relationship between God and the Jewish people. In Christ, new equal positions of chosenness came into existence between the Jewish Christians and the Gentile Christians. The following thoughts are contained in footnote nine, "The middle wall of partition between Jews and Gentiles has been broken down. God sees no racial barriers from His throne." The Apostle Paul amplifies this fact and provides a marvelous understanding which he conveyed to the predominantly Gentile audience to whom he preached.

DOES JACOB'S TROUBLE WEAR A CROSS?

> Therefore remember, that you, once Gentiles
> in the flesh--who are called Uncircumcision by
> what is called the Circumcision made in the flesh
> by hands--that at that time you were without
> Christ, being aliens from the commonwealth of
> Israel and strangers from the covenants of
> promise, having no hope and without God in the
> world. But now in Christ Jesus you who once
> were far off have been brought near by the blood
> of Christ. For He Himself is our peace, who has
> made both one, and has broken down the middle
> wall of separation . . . so as to create in Himself
> one new man from the two, thus making peace
> (Ephesians 2:11-15).

The goal of all Christians today should be to make everyone else jealous of their special, intimate relationship with God in Christ. This special bond should lead non-Christians to feel jealous, not inferior. The Jew should be jealous of the Christian's love relationship with God, not because it is exclusive, but because it is wonderful and desirable. God's call to glory and peace in Christ was to the Jews first, and then it was extended to the Greeks and other Gentiles (Romans 2:10). Today's Jews should become jealous of the love of God, not hated by the "other" people of God because Jesus will hold every hateful person in contempt.

The call of all Christians is to have such an endearing, winsome, admirable character of love that others will want to imitate their behavior and experience their relationship with their God of love. Paul's message to the Church explained God's intention for Christian/Jewish relations. "Did not Israel know? First Moses says: '*I will provoke you to jealousy by those who are not a nation*, I will move you to anger by a foolish nation'" (italics mine, Romans 10:19). God opened His heart to the Gentiles,

> I say then, Have they [the Jews] stumbled that they should fall? Certainly not! But through their fall, *to provoke them to jealousy*, salvation has come to the Gentiles (italics mine, Romans 11:11).

All Christian brothers and sisters share the high calling of God in Jesus to love the Jewish people. Christians must set out to understand and accomplish this goal within their Christian existence. The Jews must be provoked to jealousy. The Jews will identify the endearing relationship to God that genuine Christians experience and cherish. This may be the finest method to touch the Jews. God has called the Gentile Church to provoke His chosen people to jealousy. God, unlike many in the Church, has not abandoned the Jewish people.

As shown by Paul's letter to the Romans, the fall of the Jews was for the Gentile's salvation. The Gentile Church has failed to show its appreciation. Generally, it is not recognized by the Church that the salvation of the Gentiles should lead to the redemption of the Jews. Unbelieving Jews do not sin alone when rejecting God's will. Anti-Semitic Christians also reject God's will when they fail to love the Jewish people. Christians should show their joy in Christ by sharing His love with His people. Instead, they have rejected His people, and therefore rejected God's will and command to love. The Church has not been commissioned to harm the Jews because of a few wicked leaders who conspired to kill Jesus. The Church should show the path of life in Christ to the Jews in a genuine display of tolerance, appreciation, and enthusiastic Christian love. Sacrificial love was shown by God to the world, no less will call the Jews to sing accompaniment in that life of praise that is deserved by the Jewish Messiah!

THE GROWTH OF ANTI-SEMITISM IN THE CHURCH OF THE NEW WORLD

CHAPTER XII

ESCAPE FROM A CHRISTIAN WORLD?

America was a haven to persecuted people. America was a virtuous nation formed by virtuous people. Risk-taking, pioneering, hard-working folk who had been persecuted for their religious beliefs fled to America to spread their love and share their freedom. They were fueled by admirable ideals and their Christian ethos. God-fearing Christian people built the new land assuring themselves that they would preserve their freedom to worship.

The above view encapsulates one commonly held view of America by Americans. This has been the dominant view among patriots and evangelicals who are sometimes one and the same. A need exists to demythologize the New World of freedom. A rediscovery of Columbus' America is in order.

Rediscovering America

Christopher Columbus merely discovered an island in the Bahamas, not America. He called the natives "Indians," because until his death in 1506, he was convinced that he had found the East Indies. Each October, Americans celebrate a holiday which details to the children how Columbus discovered America. However, they should also be told that "In the century after Columbus' landfall, nearly ninety percent of the Native American population perished."[76] Another facet of the New World's heritage suggests that

> By 1592, a combination of disease, enslavement, and armed Spanish aggression had reduced the civilization of the Arawaks in Hispaniola from about five million people to 250.[77]

Columbus would not have been a hero to the 250 Arawaks, or the surviving ten percent remnant of the American Indians. Then again, the winners write the history books. Columbus is only a hero within a limited perspective.

---

[76] Thomas A. Bailey, and David M. Kennedy, *The American Pageant, A History of the Republic, Vol. I*, (D. C. Heath and Company, Lexington, Massachusetts, 1991), p. 10.

[77] Ibid.

If one believes that Europe had religious interests at heart in their conquest of the brave New World of America, more myths need to crumble. First, toward errors in American ethnocentrism, by "1574, thirty-three years before the first primitive English shelters in Virginia, there were about two hundred Spanish cities and towns in North and South America."[78] Obviously, America was not the first civilized society of the Americas. Toward the correction of Christian ethnocentrism, it becomes imperative to understand that by that same time, a "total of 160,000 Spanish inhabitants, mostly men, had subjugated some 5 million Indians--all in the name of the gentle Jesus."[79] It is obvious that the Spanish "Christians" had never considered provoking their converts to jealousy.

The New World was not formed in a vacuum. In the beginning, the Old World sent out missionaries and explorers. These expeditions were not led by those who were only interested in religious freedom. If the historicity of Columbus' exploits are not accurate, one point in particular is relevant to this study in Christian anti-Semitism. The day he sailed on his famous trip was a famous day for Jews. It was August 2, 1492, "The ninth of Av in the Jewish calendar. It was always kept as a day of

---

[78] Ibid., pp. 12, 13.

[79] Ibid.

fasting and mourning for the destruction of the Temple."[80] This holiday may also have been relevant to Columbus. In the year 1492 the last Jews were expelled from Spain if they refused forced conversion.

New Christians, Temporary Security

Conversion, however, offered only a temporary solution for the Jews.

The numerous conversions of Jews created a new problem for Spanish society and for the Church. Suddenly a substantial number of "New Christians" were to be found in society, no longer subject to the social, ecclesiastical, and legal disabilities of Jews but clearly of Jewish descent and often of Jewish upbringing. Their allegiance to Christianity could reasonably be questioned, since in most cases their conversion had been far from spontaneous.[81]

These Jews were then grouped into a new category known as New Christians.

These New Christians themselves showed little desire to be assimilated to the majority. They kept their identity as a distinct group, frequently retaining their ties with other Jews. They were suspected, often rightly, of holding on

---

[80] Nicholls, p. 266.

[81] Ibid., p. 262.

as best they could to their old faith and practicing it in secret.[82]

This behavior should not have surprised the Gentile leadership. Secret worship versus public confession has been a problem for Jews for many centuries.[83] Being aware of this, the Gentile Christians in Spanish society began to distrust and hate the New Christians.

Several decades after the mass, forced conversions of 1391, these New Christians began to fall into disfavor. Many of them became too successful. They competed for financial and social prominence with Christians of Gentile

---

[82] Ibid.

[83] When I was growing up, my dad and I would periodically go for walks together. Judaism and Jewish persecution was often a topic. He always wanted me to know who I was as a Jew. He also wanted me to know who our friends and enemies were. His background had proven to him that we could only depend on God and other Jews. I think he sometimes wondered how "friendly" God had been. In any case, I remember a specific question he asked me on one of those walks: "If the Nazi's came pounding on the door, and they demanded to know if there were any Jews in the house, what would you answer?" With all of my young Jewish zeal, I told him that I'd tell them the truth. "Of course, I am a Jew." He promptly scolded me suggesting that a lie would be a better answer in that vicious dilemma. It would be more valorous to deny my faith, because, I could say I was not a Jew but continue to worship in secret. He instructed me that "If you tell the truth, you will only be one more dead Jew." In contrast, I believe that Christianity does demand a different response. If Jesus, the Apostles, and the martyrs of the early Church are to be our examples, I believe that Christianity requires death before denial. If one's Christian faith is not worth dying for, it is probably not worth living for!

origin. Soon, Spain's social conscience began to identify that if the New Christians had not converted, they would have not been able to participate and compete for wealth, influence, and affluence. It was a short leap of logic to discredit them from doing so as New Christians by remembering that they were little more than "Jews in Christian clothing." By discrediting successful New Christians who had acquired status in spite of their Jewish background, the Spanish Gentiles narrowed the opportunities for aggressive competition. By the 1430's, the sentiment had further deteriorated. Jews could not avoid being hated, regardless of their belief system. Jewish New Christians were scorned and treated as though they were "masquerading around as New Christians, they had fastened themselves upon the backs of true Christians in addition to committing the religious crimes of heresy and blasphemy."[84]

Mala Sangre

The Jewish Christians and Jews of Spain came under severe anti-Semitic persecution.

A new concept now appeared, without precedent in Christian history. From the middle

---

[84] Faber, p. 6. For more information see: Henry Kamen, *Inquisition and Society in Spain in the Sixteenth and Seventeenth Centuries* (Bloomington: Indiana University Press, 1985), 20-22.

of the century, some Spanish religious orders
began to require the qualification of *limpiezza de
sangre* (i.e., Christian descent on both sides), and
they continued to require it until the nineteenth
century.[85]

The phrase suggested that without having been born
of two Christian parents, the individual had *mala sangre*,
or bad blood. Jesus, Himself would have been guilty of
mala sangre. Incredibly, this did not deter the Gentile
Christian leaders from imposing the extra-biblical
qualifications.

The purposes of regulating the opportunities of the
Jews were not designed to spread the Christian faith.
Spain's interests were not that noble. More concern was
focused on protecting the wealth of Spain's Gentile
Christians. Spanish Jews became known as *Marranos*.
That name is still spoken of among Spanish Jews.
Unfortunately it is a very derogatory term. Like the same
Italian word, it probably meant "swine." The *Marranos*
endured the horribly violent religious enterprises of the
Dominican Tomas de Torquemada from 1483. He had
been named

Inquisitor-General of both Aragon and
Castile. His name has become legendary for
ruthless zeal in the prosecution of heresy. It has
been suggested that his zeal against the New
Christians can be traced to his own Jewish

---

[85] Nicholls, p. 263

descent. However, his Jewish origins have not been convincingly demonstrated.[86]

Wandering Jews?

An interesting possibility regarding the background of Christopher Columbus should be questioned. Perhaps Columbus was interested in religious freedom in addition to discovering a shorter route to the Indies. This consideration is relevant to a research project on anti-Semitism because some would contend that Christopher Columbus had Jewish roots.[87]

There is evidence that many of Columbus' crew, including perhaps himself, were New Christians hoping to find a freer life. Indeed, the whole expedition seems to have been their enterprise, both in its planning and financing. It was largely funded by Luis de Santangel, a financier of New Christian extraction, and a principal patron was Gabriel Sanchez, High Treasurer of Aragon, himself of full Jewish descent.[88]

---

[86] Ibid. p.264.

[87] Jane Frances Amler has written another work discussing the subject. *Christopher Columbus' Jewish Roots,* available through The Jewish Book Club, Allentown, PA.

[88] Nicholls., p. 266. The author listed two references he had examined. These included: Abba Eban, *My People*, new ed. (New York: Behrman House and Random House, 1968; paperback edition,

These fascinating pieces of information will probably never be touted in the Columbus Day festivities, however, parades are not always based upon truth. In the case of Spain's explorers and Europe's effort to win the New World, the truth may be more fascinating than myth. Jewish planning, Jewish money, and potentially Jewish sailors had much of the responsibility for the discovery of America.

One, even more astounding fact should be realized.

At least one Jew was on board, Luis de Torres, an interpreter. The first European to set foot on American soil, de Torres was a descendant of a long line of Sephardim (Jews of Spain and Portugal).[89]

Luis de Torres, a Sephardic Jew, was the first European white man to stand in America. However, he was not the last Jew to come to this New World from Spain.

Persecution convinced many oppressed Jews to leave Spain, and, later, similar negative incentives paved the way for future emigration. The story of how these unwanted

---

1984), p. 196 and *The Enlightened: the writings of Luis de Carvajal el Mozo,* ed., trans., and with an introduction by Seymour B. Liebman (Coral Gables, FL: University of Miami Press, 1967).

[89] Kenneth Libo, and Irving Howe, *We lived There Too,* (St. Martin's/Marek, New York, 1984), p.39.

souls landed in America is worthy of note, as is the story of their welcome to the land of freedom.

<u>Portuguese "Evangelism"</u>

Many Jews fled to Portugal during the Spanish Inquisition in 1492. "Mass conversion, rather than expulsion, put an end to Portuguese Jewry. No known Jews remained in Portugal by 1497."[90] It is revolting to think that all the Jews of a nation could be violently driven away, forcefully converted, or killed. Nonetheless, all of the Jews of Portugal vanished in the name of love. This occurred as a result of the love of Portugal's King Manuel for a Spanish princess. Portugal's anti-Jewish laws were enacted in an effort to pacify the king of Spain. He was not comfortable with Manuel's level of tolerance toward the Jews in Portugal. To win that lady of Spain, Manuel intensified Jewish oppression. Previously, Manuel had been quite tolerant of the 100,000 Jews and New Christians that had emigrated from Spain.

Manuel adopted a policy of forced conversion in preference to expulsion. During 1497, Jews, both children and adults, were physically dragged into Church and forcibly baptized. Others voluntarily accepted Christianity in order to remain in the country and escape

---

[90] Nicholls, p. 266.

enslavement to the monarch, the penalty for accepting neither expulsion nor conversion.[91]

Religious persecution plagued other parts of Christian Europe; Jews were not the only victims. Spain's despicable actions against Jews through the Church were similar to the situation faced by the Puritans in England, and the Huguenots in France.[92]

---

[91] Faber, p. 6.

[92] The Huguenots were fiercely calvinistic Protestants living in France. On St. Bartholomew's Day in the year of 1572, the Roman Catholics barbarously slaughtered over 10,000 of these French Protestants.

CHAPTER XIII

OLD PROBLEMS IN A NEW WORLD

Hated, displaced religious "outsiders" looked for new lands to escape the horrible persecution from the domineering, violent, insecure "insiders." Many Jews of the Expulsion, as it is known, came to the New World. "Nevertheless, the Inquisition pursued the New Christian exiles to the Spanish dominions in the New World and many perished there."[93] No place was truly safe for a Jew.

The first Jews to arrive in territory now included in the United States came from South America in 1654. They were refugees from the persecution that began in Spain and Portugal and spread to the South American colonies.[94]

---

[93] Nicholls, p. 266.

[94] Conrad Hoffman Jr., _What Now for the Jews? A Challenge to the Christian Conscience,_ (Friendship Press, New York, 1948), P. 31.

DOES JACOB'S TROUBLE WEAR A CROSS?

America had its first Jews, and with them, America had a new "lower class of citizenry." They were not welcomed into America with the other freedom-minded pioneers. They did not fit in, but they were not alone.

Not the Land of the Free

William Penn had formed his new colony for the benefit of persecuted Quakers. Penn was more liberal than most of the early colonial leaders. Pennsylvania did permit freedom of worship, even for people who worshipped differently. Mr. Penn, however, "under pressure from London, was forced to deny Catholics and Jews the privilege of voting or holding office."[95]

Even before the Quaker's established Pennsylvania, another religious group was seeking freedom to worship in 1634. The fourth English colony to be established was Maryland. Lord Baltimore hoped to prosper financially in his adventurous endeavor in the New World, but he also intended to form a safe haven for the religious freedom of Roman Catholicism. America had plenty of room to permit the religious faithful to carve out a resting place from the turmoil of hatred across the sea. "Lord Baltimore, a canny soul, permitted unusual freedom of worship at the

---

[95] Ibid., p. 40.

outset."[96]   In 1649, they passed the famed famous Act of Toleration. "Maryland's new religious statute guaranteed toleration to all Christians. But it decreed the death penalty for those, like Jews and Atheists, who denied the divinity of Jesus.[97]"

This Act of Toleration was not tolerant; nonetheless, it became the law of Maryland. For obvious reasons, Maryland did not give rise to an early Jewish population.

As stated above, American Jews were not greeted with a warm welcome in Maryland, and Pennsylvania was not formed until 1681. Some Jews did arrive in America before William Penn became a Quaker in 1660. One destination for those Jewish settlers was Rhode Island. This little state was actually founded by an extreme Puritan Separatist. He wanted to see the Puritans make a clean break with the Church of England. Roger Williams was exiled from the Massachusetts Bay Colony in 1635 by less radical Puritans. He obtained help from some Indians and established a settlement in Providence. There he built the first Baptist Church in America. Mr. Williams is to be applauded because after he suffered persecution at the hands of the religious leaders, "He established complete freedom of religion, even for Jews and Catholics."[98]   This

---

[96] Bailey and Kennedy, p. 18.

[97] Ibid.

[98] Ibid., p. 33.

man was far ahead of his time. Williams was unique for many years in his posture towards true religious freedom in America. Unfortunately, the rest of the people of the area ridiculed his efforts. Rhode Island became known as "Rogues" Island and the "sewer" because of its true toleration and their willingness to admit undesirables. The religious folk of snobbish Boston, unwelcome at home in England, forgot the feelings they had experienced when they were not welcome and were compelled to look for freedom in America.

As previously discussed, to avoid persecution, death, or forced conversion during the Spanish Inquisition, many Jews left Spain. The Christians drove them out but failed to offer them viable alternative destinations. Large numbers of Jewish families uprooted by Christian hatred were forced to choose other directions for searching out new lives. "Most of those expelled from the Iberian Peninsula made their way south to North Africa and then eastward. Some turned northward to the Netherlands."[99] They ventured away in an effort to begin new lives in the New World. They journeyed toward freedom a hemisphere away.

Many of the Jews came to South America. These Jews became some of the first European settlers in Brazil.

---

[99] Nicholls, p. 266.

When Portugal gained control of Brazil in 1580, the Jews were uprooted again. Their memories had been seared by the flames of Christian hatred in Portugal. Once more they were faced with the problems of the Inquisition in their new land.

The chosen people seemed to be chosen to suffer. They were chosen to flee and chosen to be uprooted while remaining wandering Jews.[100]

---

[100] Credit is due Portugal's King Manuel. Although he was not without guilt in his behavior toward the Jews, compared to his contemporaries and successors, Manuel was far more reasonable. Manuel realized that those Jews who had come to Portugal were not likely to truly convert to Christianity. He understood that since these Jews had already resisted conversion in Spain under the threats they experienced, it was not likely that they would simply have a change of heart. "In 1497, for example, the Crown proclaimed that for twenty years there were to be no prosecutions for religious offenses and that offenders were thereafter to be prosecuted by civil rather than ecclesiastical authorities." This prohibited the religious zealots from delivering punishments based upon their intolerant views. Manuel also harshly repressed the massacres of New Christians in the early 1500's. Later, in 1512, he added the crime of heresy to the list of religious offenses which would not be prosecuted for twenty years. This offered a time of healing to the persecuted Jews who would have previously been classed as heretics and punished immediately. All of these measures permitted Jews to secretly remain Jewish, with less fear of reprisal. It is unfortunate, but this more open treatment of Jews in Portugal ended within ten years after King Manuel died in 1521. From then the tide turned against Jews more violently in Portugal. "Through papal proclamations in 1536, 1539, and 1547, an Inquisition modeled after that in Spain was created in Portugal." Quotes and additional information on this subject material come from Faber, p. 7.

Haven in Brazil

Their wandering led them to a short lived haven. In 1630, the Dutch conquered the state of Pernambuco and the Jews of Brazil were free again. "By 1645, close to fifteen hundred Jews resided in Dutch Brazil. Two religious congregations were established, one of which (Recife's) employed the first rabbi in the New World."[101]

They flourished in the port town of Recife. This city with its own harbor proved to be a haven of freedom for nearly one thousand Jewish residents. There, a familiar Jewish lifestyle was "complete with a synagogue, a rabbi, doctors, lawyers, peddlers, merchants--and even a main street called *Rua dos Judeos* (Street of the Jews).

Once more, a Jew did not have to fear being a Jew in the New World."[102] Their freedom did not endure for long. The Portuguese came back in 1654 and reconquered Brazil. This caused the Jews of the area to flee to safer ground. Relentless upheavals must have brought times of hopelessness to these Jews in Brazil. Tragedy seemed to follow these first Jews of the New World. Suffering seemed to be an inherited characteristic, passed down from every generation which preceded them.

------

[101] Faber, p. 11.

[102] Libo and Howe, p. 40.

Pirates, Privateers, and Providence

An interesting vignette of what transpired in 1654 can be successfully traced back to that time. Sixteen boats carried the nearly one thousand Jewish refugees from Brazil to "safety." The vessels of mercy took different directions. Some of the Jews on board were probably weary of trying to chisel out a life in the rock-hard temperament of an unforgiving New World full of old pains. Some of them may have desperately wanted to go home to the Old World of Europe. Some had their hopes pinned to a destination in Holland where the Jews enjoyed a semblance of religious and economic freedom. Others had visions of glory in seeking newer worlds. These traveled to Caribbean colonies controlled by the Dutch, French, or English. Sixteen ships left Recife bound for freedom. To their bad fortune, one was captured by a Spanish pirate ship. To their good fortune, the Spanish pirate ship was captured by a French privateer. The French vessel was called the *St. Charles*. In this good-news-bad-news scenario, the French vessel carried them to the Dutch West Indies trading colony of New Amsterdam (which later became better known as New York). The good news was that they landed in a colony under the control of Holland. The bad news was that they were placed into the hands of the infamous Peter Stuyvesant. Stuyvesant was a strong-willed Christian who hated Jews.

Apparently, God had an elaborate plan. Hatred certainly played a part in the results of the plan but most sadly, many Christians seemed to ignore that God is love. Though they tried, Christians could not overcome providence in keeping the Jews out of America. In practical terms the Church in early America had no love for the Jewish people.

America's Welcome

Twenty-three Jewish people came to New Amsterdam to start America's first permanent Jewish settlement. They arrived on September 7, in time to celebrate Rosh Hashanah (the Jewish New Year) which fell on September 12 in 1654.[103] The excitement felt by the travel-worn Jewish pilgrims can only be imagined. They were in search of a new "promise land." The enthusiasm of these tired mothers and fathers had risen as they shared their hope with their weary, anxious children. They envisioned a new life, in a new land, wherein they intended to celebrate their New Year's rituals with new hope.

However, Stuyvesant "started a campaign to drive the Jews out of New Amsterdam. Already predisposed by a strict Calvinist upbringing to look upon Jews as killers of

---

[103] Faber, p. 145.

Christ,"[104] he wrote a letter to his superior in Holland. The anti-Semitic zeal is unmistakable. He explained his reasons for forcing the expulsion of the unwelcome Jews.

> The Jews who have arrived would nearly all like to remain here, but learning that they (with their customary usury and deceitful trading with the Christians) were repugnant to the inferior magistrates, as also to the people having most affection for you; the Deaconry also fearing that owing to their present indigence they might become a charge in the coming winter, we have for the benefit of this weak and newly developing land, deemed it useful to require them in a friendly way to depart; praying also most seriously in this connection, for ourselves as also for the general community of your worships, that the deceitful race--such hateful blasphemers of the name of Christ--be not allowed further to infect and trouble the new colony.[105]

The leaders in Holland who answered his letter agreed with Stuyvesant showing their own anti-Semitic feelings in their written response.

> We would have liked to effectuate and fulfill your wishes that the new territories should no more be allowed to be infected by people of the Jewish nation, for we foresee therefrom the same difficulties which you fear.[106]

---

[104] Libo and Howe, p. 41.

[105] Ibid., pp. 41-42.

[106] Ibid.

However, there were other factors to consider. The Dutch had suffered a great loss at the hands of the Portuguese when they lost Brazil. This worked to the advantage of the displaced Jews. Fortunately for the struggling Jews in America, some prosperous Dutch Jews owned stock in the trading company that had established Stuyvesant's settlement. Headquarters did not want to risk raising the ire of the Jewish shareholders. The twenty-three Jews which had landed and remained in America, stayed, in spite of the prevailing twisted Christian attitudes. In that situation, a few well placed shares of Jewish controlled stock went further than the commands of love from Jesus to His flock.

Stuyvesant's attempt to deport the Jews was not the last dilemma faced by the earliest Jewish settlers. Jews were prohibited from participating in the basic freedoms of the land. They could not vote or own property in Amsterdam. Employment and travel were restricted and controlled. Like the Old Testament prophet Daniel in his strange new world under Gentile domination, Jews were prohibited from praying in public.

The perils of the New World presented new opportunities for anti-Semitic Christians to discriminate against Jews. Some of their methods had not yet been considered in Europe. In New Amsterdam, the Jews were not permitted to "stand guard against Indian attacks on the grounds that they were 'not admitted or counted among the citizens.'" This law was later successfully challenged.

Asser Levy, a native of New Amsterdam, together with Jacob Barsimson petitioned for the right to stand guard like other settlers. Though they were turned down initially, in 1655 Levy acquired this right, thus opening the way for full citizenship rights for Jews in the New World.[107]

No Place To Run

Circumstances were very bad in New Amsterdam for these Jews. They would probably have left the area if it were not for several deterring factors. Christians seemed to hate Jews wherever they were. Violence was being felt by Jews in other parts of the world. "In Spain and Portugal, Jews were still being burned at the stake for refusing to renounce their faith."[108] An incredible carnage of Polish Jews took place as they were forcibly locked between Catholic and Greek Orthodox "love." A sample of why Jews looked for asylum in the middle seventeenth century can be seen from Christian treatment in Europe.

Estates were devastated, manor-houses reduced to ashes, and human beings barbarously done to death. The victims were flayed and burned alive, mutilated and left to the agony of a

---

[107] Ibid., p. 43.

[108] Ibid., p. 45.

lingering death. Infants were slit like fish or slaughtered at the breasts of their mothers or cast alive into wells. Women were ripped open and then sewed up again with live cats thrust into their bowels; many married or unmarried, were violated before the eyes of their menfolk, and those that were comely were carried away.[109]

The treatment was abominable. Worldwide, the Jewish people were being devastated under the banner of Christianity. A place of Jewish refuge was tremendously necessary.

In Poland in 1648 and 1649, over 100,000 Jews were murdered and their communities destroyed by Chmielnicki's bloodthirsty Cossacks. In England after hundreds of years of banishment, Jews were still forbidden legal entry. Nor were Jews any more welcome in colonial Virginia where the Church of England held sway.[110]

Jewish lives were at risk in Maryland due to anti-Semitic laws. The Christian Puritans of New England viewed the Jews as a fallen people without hope. It did not appear that they intended to offer any hope to the Jewish settlers. The Jews in the fledgling "Land of Freedom" were simply not welcome. An exception to this mistreatment occurred in the "sewer" of Rhode Island, where some Jews also settled.

---

[109] Margolis and Marx, p. 552.

[110] Libo, and Howe, p. 45.

One Rhode Island settlement was started in approximately 1658. Fifteen Jewish families eventually tried settling in Newport, Rhode Island. They heard of the religious tolerance which existed in Rhode Island, and they came from Barbados. Little is known about this settlement. However, it has been documented that the Jews of Newport purchased land for a cemetery. This was one of the practical requirements for a Jewish community. It is known that they were involved in some level of commerce because two law suits for alleged infractions of the English Navigation Acts were recorded against Jews in the area in 1684 and 1685. By 1770, as many as thirty Jewish households existed in Newport. Part of this growth resulted after a terrible epidemic infected much of Curacao. Some of these folk emigrated to Newport from that island. In 1763, the Jewish families of Newport constructed a synagogue.

> Unfortunately, the congregation was not to enjoy it for long. As in New York, the occupation of the city by the British in 1776 prompted most of the members to leave, an event from which the community recovered only briefly during the 1780's.[111]

Ultimately, this Jewish settlement failed to endure as a lasting community for Jewish life in early America.

---

[111] Faber, p. 38.

DOES JACOB'S TROUBLE WEAR A CROSS?

The Jewish people came to America by no plan of their own. Spanish pirates set the course for Jewish emigration. The reason the first American Jews escaped a sea-going inquisition was due to providence and a French privateer. The motivating factor of the privateer was his hope to profit 2,500 guilders for delivering the Jewish passengers to the only place that would begrudgingly take them.[112] <u>America was the land of the free, but freedom was reserved for white Christians</u>.

<u>English Grace</u>

In 1664, England successfully captured New Amsterdam. They ultimately named it in honor of the Duke of York, brother of King Charles II. New York continued to prohibit public worship by Jews, but they did permit settlement. Once there, the Jews found a way to circumvent such laws, for as early as 1692 mention is made in a public document of a Jewish house of worship in New York. In a map dated 1695 a site on Beaver Street is referred to as "the Jewes Synagogue."[113]

---

[112] Faber suggests on page 29 of his work that due to the poverty of the Jewish passengers the captain of the vessel was ultimately forced to sue his Jewish passengers for payment.

[113] Libo and Howe, p. 45.

One effect of England's success in taking New York turned out to be an improvement for Jews living there. Oliver Cromwell permitted a more open view toward the Jews of England around the time of 1655. Tolerance toward the Jewish residents of the English colonies of the New World became more evident as a result of the general changes experienced by Jews in England.

> In 1655, the Jews dispatched Rabbi Menashe Ben Israel to London to negotiate with Oliver Cromwell's government for the admission of Jews. Cromwell's government informally responded affirmatively, whether motivated by the prospect of enhancing England's commercial prowess or by the Puritan postulate that the advent of the millennium required first the conversion of the Jews. By 1660, approximately thirty-five Sephardic families had taken up residence . . . but by the middle of the eighteenth century, when seven thousand to eight thousand Jews resided in England.[114]

Whether the motivation stemmed from selfish reasoning, true tolerance, evangelistic zeal, or jealousy, is an unanswered question. Nonetheless, the position of the Jews in New York did improve. After the turn of the century, tolerance toward Jews in England improved even more.

---

[114] Faber, p. 15.

DOES JACOB'S TROUBLE WEAR A CROSS?

> English Jews could reside anywhere without restriction, employ Christian servants, and enter the professions. They enjoyed equality under the law with Protestants, paid the same taxes, could serve as constables and soldiers, and shared guard duty in the city of London. . . . Supported generally by the Crown, the great landowners, and liberal economic thinkers who believed that a Jewish presence contributed to the nation's wealth, the Jews of England also benefited from the Christian theory that their conversion, supposedly a prelude to the millennium, could best be effected by welcoming them and integrating them into society.[115]

This wellspring of "Christian love" did not carry the Jews into the loving arms of Gentile England for very long.

> Fearful of their competition, the merchants of the City of London limited the number of Jewish brokers to a maximum of twelve, excluded them from the Levant and the Russia trading companies, helped defeat the Jewish Naturalization Bill of 1753, and prevented them from opening retail shops in the City by requiring a Christian oath for admission to freemanship.[116]

New York was home to over twenty Jewish families in 1695. The Jewish population grew slowly, but continuously. By 1800, it is estimated that America was

---

[115] Faber, p. 94.

[116] Ibid., p. 96.

home to 2,000 Jews. The improving, more tolerant posture toward Jews in England brought additional benefits to the English colony of New York.

The despised Christian oaths required for freemanship in England were still required in Rhode Island as late as 1762. The unsuccessful appeal to the Rhode Island superior court prohibited two Jewish merchants from obtaining citizenship in that colony and proved the oaths were required by "citing the inadmissibility of Jews to freemanship in Rhode Island because of the colony's origins as a settlement for 'the free and quiet enjoyment of the Christian religion and a desire of propagating the same.'"[117] The same oaths were not forced upon Jews in New York where one of the Jewish merchants later settled. This and other developments gave the Jews in New York unprecedented opportunities for growth in their Jewish community. Soon, America did begin to look like a new promise land for Jews in America.

---

[117] Ibid., pp. 97-98.

CHAPTER XIV

THE PROMISE LAND

Postrevolutionary America did become a haven for Jews. Much of this change was due to the changing Christian position toward the need to see Jews converted to Christianity. This atmosphere within the Church led to appeals in the secular world to accept Jews into society. Although it was intended as a means to make Christianity more appealing to Jews, doubtless, this type of acceptance did manifest a more favorable situation for Jews in general. Christianity's character of love was certainly more appealing than whips, chains, or lynch mobs.

The Jewish population benefited not only from the rule of religious toleration in postrevolutionary America but also from the theological proposition that accepting Jews in society would hasten their conversion. Although this premise implied that Judaism was a transitory phenomenon, the doctrine did benefit Jews by

> justifying a benevolent attitude toward them
> among the Christian majority.[118]

The intent of the change may have been less important than the change itself. For whatever reason, the Jewish people were finally given an opportunity to secure a place for themselves in the land and history of early America.

Colonial Jews distinguished themselves in military service, commerce, shipping, civic service, and even in the politics of colonial America. Modern Jewish Americans are proud of various accomplishments that the early Jewish patriots made to their nation. Those Jews who joined the struggle against English domination were valued as members of a precious minority of Americans. The highly revered American Revolution was not highly revered by all Americans. Actually, that great revolution which introduced Democracy to the modern world was not a unified effort. John Adams is credited with reporting that only one third of the colonials supported America's quest for independence from England.

> The brutal truth is that only a select minority
> of the American colonials attached themselves to
> the cause of independence with a spirit of selfless
> devotion . . . these were the freedom-loving

---

118 Ibid., p. 131.

patriots who deserved the gratitude and esteem of generations yet unborn.[119]

It is likely that two thirds of the citizenry did not support the war effort. The romanticized, imaginative view of the American Revolution, passed down in revised fashion to glorify the American ethos, is simply not accurate. Among the minority who did support the successful revolt, Jewish freedom fighters provided much needed support. Clearly, the Jews of America have been good for America.

Jewish patriots offered much support in the fight for independence. In addition to revolutionary soldiers, the American war effort needed guns and supplies to function effectively. One example of Jewish involvement in aiding the cause of freedom can be seen in the accomplishments of the Gratz family[120] of Pennsylvania. The Jewish share of privateering, which occurred to the benefit of the American troops, has been estimated to be six percent of the total during the war years. This percentage of involvement from the Jewish colonials was, "far out of proportion to its tiny population."[121] Michael Gratz had

---

[119] Bailey and Kennedy, p. 119.

[120] Interestly, Thomas Jefferson actually wrote the Declaration of Independence in a house that the Gratz family eventually turned into a store. This building was located on Market Street in Philadelphia. Libo and Howe, p. 76.

[121] Libo and Howe, p. 76.

been chosen to locate and acquire the clothes and blankets needed for the troops by Philadelphia's Committee of Safety. He also supplied the blockade runners on the Potomac River to gain needed goods from the world beyond Philadelphia. As the war continued, Michael Gratz's brother performed services that were needed to sustain the war effort. "Barnard supplied the Continental Army with rifles (manufactured by Joseph Simon), ammunition drums, blankets, and food."[122]

The level of important activities accomplished by Jewish Americans was substantial.[123] Had this revolution been lost, the Jews would not have gained the opportunities and respect which led to their modern day level of success. What has been achieved by the Jews in this present era of religious freedom would have been unlikely. More likely, they would have simply been hung along with the other traitors to the Crown.

---

[122] Ibid.

[123] For more details on the contributions of Jews in American history, an excellent source is the five volume work, *The Jewish People In America*, a Series Sponsored by the American Jewish Historical Society, edited by Henry F. Feingold, published by The Johns Hopkins University Press, 1992.

As in the American Revolution, the difference between a revolt and a revolution is usually determined by who won. The history books that record the victory are generally flavored by the political leanings of the victors. As has been suggested, "the winners write the history books." Some may call this the sweetened version of the facts, "revisionist history" if the facts change and dramatically drift away from the truth.[124] In like fashion, Americans have been subjected to a view of their own history colored by patriotic emotions and political biases. These sentiments help stir a Fourth of July parade but are unlikely to generate historically accurate commentaries on the past. When the knowledge of a grievous past error is lost, the error is likely to be repeated.

---

[124] In American history, errors have abounded on issues related to the Civil War. The South is generally portrayed as having illegally broken the bond with the North over the immoral issue of slavery. The victorious North produced much of the literature and historical accounts to preserve the drama. Unfortunately, in their accounts, they were prone to "forgetting" the true rights of sovereignty held by those southern states. Actually, the southern states had won their freedom as part of the original thirteen colonies. Therefore, they were legally identified as independent. A very persuasive argument can be made suggesting that history would be better represented if it was "remembered" that the Southern states left the Union legally. Many Southerners believed they were illegally invaded by the North. The issue of Slavery (though sinful and horrid) was potentially less troublesome to the adversaries than the issue of state's rights. Still, many Americans probably identify slavery as the singular issue that split the nation.

DOES JACOB'S TROUBLE WEAR A CROSS?

Perhaps it was best related by the Jewish philosopher, Baruch Spinoza. He said. "If you want the present to be different from the past, study the past."

CHAPTER XV

JUDAISM WILL ENDURE

One must wonder whether modern American Christians have a higher view of Jews and Judaism than postrevolutionary American Christians. Consider a quote from chapter eleven.

> The Jewish population benefited not only from the rule of religious toleration in postrevolutionary America but also from the theological proposition that accepting Jews in society would hasten their conversion. Although this premise implied that Judaism was a transitory phenomenon, the doctrine did benefit Jews by justifying a benevolent attitude toward them among the Christian majority.

Kind gestures and words aimed at persuasion, even when that persuasion is orthodox and evangelistic, should be questioned. Larry Hill, a veteran missionary and missions professor encourages all Christians to remember that, "To Jesus, people were not 'targets.' In order for

evangelism to take place, there has to be incarnation."[125]
God meets men at man's level through His immortal Spirit.
Jesus touches non-Christians while living through
Christians. Neither Jews nor Gentiles should be treated as
"targets" for conversion. Rather, unbelievers of every
background should be seen as potential friends, people to
serve, and carriers of certain burdens that only God can lift.
Christians should walk in the Spirit so that the
"incarnation" impacts the world through Christianity.
Humble servants must realize that unbelievers are
constantly in need of God.

As is evidenced by his quotes in chapter four, Luther
became frustrated with the Jews, and their resistance to
Christian conversion. Others, similarly frustrated, may
have also concluded that the Jews are beyond redemption
because they continue to reject redemption as understood
by the Church. History shows that Jews tend to remain
Jewish. The Spanish Inquisition has proven that even
forced conversions only provided more opportunities for
Jews to continue practicing Judaism. Indirectly, this book
has examined some of the reasons why evangelism has
failed within the Jewish world. Namely, Christianity has
been horribly abusive to the Jewish people, therefore,

---

[125] Quoted from a lecture at Christ For The Nations Institute
in February 1994, as written in my notes.

Gentile Christians have not provoked the Jewish people to jealousy. These facts may have led some Jews to believe that their moral standards are higher than Christian standards. Since no incentives exist to "step down" to experience a religion of lower moral character, the true nature of Christianity may be hidden from the Jews because of an incorrect belief. The orthodox Christian faith reveals the Fatherhood of God, the Kingdom of God, and the loving salvation of God. Perhaps Jewish people have not been exposed to enough examples of good Christians to realize the incredibly high moral character of Jesus and true Christianity.

A recent survey suggests that Jewish people tend to have a higher view of their moral standards than others in America. "Jewish people (41 percent) are the most likely to describe themselves as very good vs. 30 percent of Catholics and 27 percent of Protestants."[126] Jews might believe their religion helps them be good in a more effective fashion than Christianity appears to help Christians be good. This does not mean that more Jews are good or that Jews see themselves as more likely to be good than Christians. It suggests, however, that in their view, Jews might not see the need for Christianity to help them be good.

---

[126] James Patterson and Peter Kim, *The Day America Told The Truth: What People Really Believe About Everything That Really Matters,* (Prentice Hall Press, New York, 1991), p. 202.

<u>Until He Comes</u>

Judaism is not a transitory phenomenon. Quite the contrary, the alternative is no more than an obtuse, frustratingly arrogant presumption. The fact that Jews have not become extinct or evangelized is proof of their endurance. God has a people, and He has a plan for His people. Neither this writer nor future readers know God's designs. It would be presumptuous to assume that Jews are supposed to reject Judaism in favor of Christianity. Further, that would suggest that Judaism should be subordinate to Christianity. Judaism must serve a very important purpose. It has tenaciously outlived every major world religion. No other people in history continue to exist, as a people, without a national homeland. The Jewish people have existed outside of a homeland for centuries as an identifiable, individual, uniquely distinct group. The Jews survived like this (i.e., a people without a homeland) for millennia. No examples exist of any other religious-racial-national people group like the Jewish people. The Jewish religion binds Jews together. They had no homeland for 2,000 years. They spoke different languages, as they lived in different countries. Some have been white, others black, some even yellow. The only common denominators lie in their religion (although varying forms of Judaism exist) and God's choice of the Jews as His covenant people. Their survival has not been based upon their righteousness. Their survival has not been based upon their wit. Their survival has not even been based upon their unity (it is almost a proverb that two Jews will always have three opinions). No, God has unquestionably remained faithful even when they have been unfaithful. The biased worldview of Gentile Christians is subject to change. The focus and practice of Judaism is subject to change. God's choice, the "apple of His eye," and His faithfulness is unchanging.

The "time of Jacob's trouble" discussed at the beginning of this book has an end. The message God delivered through Jeremiah, however, did not end until after the deliverance of Israel, and, the punishment of Israel's enemies. In conclusion, consider God's words to the enemies of the Children of Israel.

> Therefore all they that devour thee shall be devoured, And all thine adversaries, every one of them, shall go into captivity; And they that spoil thee shall be a spoil, And all that prey upon thee will I give for a prey . . . And ye shall be My people, And I will be your God. Behold, a storm of the LORD is gone forth in fury, A sweeping storm; It shall whirl upon the head of the wicked. The fierce anger of the LORD shall not return, Until He have executed, and till He have performed the Purposes of His heart; In the end of days ye shall consider it (Jeremiah 30: 16, 22-24).

Anti-Semitism is wickedness. Anti-Semitism will bring forth the fierce anger of God. Although the Church has been a source of anti-Semitism in the past, God's love

DOES JACOB'S TROUBLE WEAR A CROSS?

demands that the love of Jesus be exhibited by all Christians toward all Jews. Baal Shem Tov was very insightful, "memory is the key." <u>God loves the Jewish people; their enemies will be His enemies</u>!

BIBLIOGRAPHY

Augustine. *The Confessions of St. Augustine.* Translated
by E. B. Pusey, New York: J. M. Dent & Sons Ltd.,
1920.

Bader, Gershom. *The Encyclopedia of Talmudic Sages.*
Translated by Solomon Katz. Northvale, New Jersey:
Jason Aronson, Inc., 1988.

Bailey, Thomas A., and David M. Kennedy. *The American
Pageant.* Vol. I. Lexington, Massachusetts: D.C.
Heath and Company, 1991.

Birnbaum, Philip. *A Book of Jewish Concepts.* New York:
Hebrew Publishing Co., 1964.

Boettner, Loraine. *The Reformed Doctrine of
Predestination.* Phillipsburg, New Jersey: Presbyterian
and Reformed Publishing Company, 1932.

Bonhoeffer, Dietrich. *The Cost of Discipleship.* New
York: Macmillan Publishing Company, 1963.

Bruce, F. F. *New Testament History.* Garden City, New
York: Doubleday-Galilee Book, 1980.

Cohen, Shaye J. D. *From the Maccabees to the Mishnah.*
Philadelphia: The Westminster Press, 1987.

Cohn-Sherbok, Dan. *The Crucified Jew: Twenty Centuries of Christian Anti-Semitism*. London: HarperCollins Publishers, 1992.

Dante. *The Divine Comedy*. A New Prose Translation by H. R. Huse. New York: Holt, Rinehart and Winston, Inc., 1954.

Dowley, Dr. Tim. Org. Ed., *Eerdman's Handbook to the History of Christianity*. Grand Rapids, Michigan: Wm. B. Eerdmans Publishing Company, 1988.

Eusebius, Pamphilus, *The Ecclesiastical History of*, Translated by Christian Frederick Cruse, Grand Rapids, Michigan, Baker Book House, 1992.

Faber, Eli. *A Time For Planting, The First Migration 1654-1820*. Baltimore, MD: The John Hopkins University Press, 1992.

Fee, Gordon and Douglas Stuart. *How to Read the Bible for All its Worth*. Grand Rapids, Michigan: Zondervan Publishing House, 1993.

Henry, Matthew. *Commentary on the Whole Bible*. Grand Rapids, Michigan: Zondervan Publishing House, Grand Rapids, Michigan, 1960.

Hoffman, Conrad Jr. *What Now for the Jews? A Challenge to the Christian Conscience*. New York: Friendship Press, 1948.

Josephus, Flavius. Translated by William Whiston, *The Works of Josephus: New Updated Edition*. Massachusetts: Hendrickson Publishers, Inc., 1993.

Libo, Kenneth, and Irving Howe. *We Lived There Too*. New York: St. Martin's / Marek, 1984.

Lindsey, Hal. *The Road To Holocaust*. New York, New York: Bantam Books, 1989.

Mack, Maynard, General Editor. *The Norton Anthology of World Masterpieces*. New York: W. W. Norton & Company, 1992.

Margolis, Max L., and Alexander Marx. *A History of the Jewish People*. New York: A Temple Book, Atheneum, 1973.

Miller, Kevin A. Christian History, "The Crusades." Carol Stream, IL: Issue 90, Volume XII, Number 4, 1993.

Nassif, Bradley. Moody Monthly, "From Kiev to the Kremlin." Chicago, IL: Moody Bible Institute, Volume 88, Number 10, June, 1988.

Nicholls, William. *Christian Antisemitism, A History of Hate*. Northvale, New Jersey: Jason Aronson, Inc., 1993.

Patterson, James, and Peter Kim. *The Day America Told The Truth: What People Really Believe About Everything That Really Matters*. New York: Prentice Hall Press, 1991.

Pentecost, J. Dwight, *Things To Come*. Grand Rapids, Michigan: Zondervan Publishing House, 1969.

Phillips, J. B. *The New Testament in Modern English*. New York: Macmillan Publishing Co., Inc., 1972.

Seif, Jeffrey, Dr. *Origin of the Christian Faith*. Dallas, Texas: JSM Publishing in cooperation with Christ For The Nations Institute, 1992.

Sparks, H. F. D., Editor. *The Apocryphal Old Testament*. Oxford: Oxford University Press, 1990.

Steinsaltz, Adin. *The Essential Talmud*. Northvale , New Jersey: Jason Aronson, Inc., 1992.

Vaughan, Curtis. *The Bible From 26 Translations*. Grand Rapids, Michigan: Baker Book House, 1988.